"Bill Smith's *Loving Well* is blessedly startling. Some people offer us devotional books about Jesus. Others give us practical tips for life. Seldom does anyone do this—giving us Jesus and his love and then showing us how we can live him out in all the hard places. Every page pushes you to live a life much bigger than yourself. I love books about Revival, when the fire finally comes down. This one blazes right now."

D. Clair Davis, DrThéol, Professor of Church History and Chaplain, Redeemer Seminary, Dallas

"Bill is the kind of Bible teacher we all need to spend more time inhabiting Scripture with—profound, but accessible; sophisticated, but humble; theologically rich, but practically oriented—and this book captures all of that. Bill consistently delivers Bible teaching and pastoral application at its very best."

The Rev. Dr. Ray Cannata, Senior Pastor, Redeemer Presbyterian Church, New Orleans

"Good Dr. Smith's book laid open my conscience with a scalpel, yet an IV of anesthesia dripped soothingly throughout. By the end, he had sewed me up and left no scar. Will you agree with every word? Maybe not . . . I didn't. But these chapters changed me. They're brilliant."

Steven Estes, Pastor; author of *Called to Die*; coauthor with Joni Eareckson Tada of *A Step Further* and *When God Weeps*

"Bill is an excellent guide in addressing the grave paucity of genuine friendships in our churches. He tells us why marriages go under, demystifies biblical counseling, provides a fresh look at the problem of evil, teaches us confronting without condemnation, and shows us how to understand conflicts as opportunities for grace. And it's all centered on the only hope we have—Jesus."

Rev. Sam A. Andreades, Pastor, the Village Church

"Through scriptural insight and stories from everyday life—including his extensive counseling experience—Bill Smith shows us why Christ's love for us is the only source of a genuine love for others. This is an honest, personal, vulnerable, hopeful, and helpful book."

Ron Lutz, Pastor, New Life Presbyterian Church, Dresher, PA

"In the introduction, Bill promises not to present Jesus merely as our example but more as the one who meets us and through our experiences of him gives us power to live a Christian life. I was not disappointed. This book is rooted in insightful exegesis and connected with real life."

Ed Jiang, Assistant Pastor at the Pittsburgh Chinese Church, Oakland, PA

"Soaked in Scripture and solidly biblical in all of its counsel, this wonderful book by a seasoned pastor and Christian counselor provides practical, Christ-centered guidance for growing authentic, vulnerable, and loving relationships."

Tara Barthel, author of *Living the Gospel in Relationships* and coauthor of *Peacemaking Women* and *Redeeming Church Conflicts*

"This is not in-the-clouds abstract theology, but in-the-trenches engagement with the gritty challenges of how to love others well. Bill Smith's disarming honesty, piercing insight, and winsome writing invite and equip the reader to love others in the same multifaceted ways God loves us."

Michael R. Emlet, MDiv, MD, faculty and counselor, Christian Counseling & Educational Foundation (CCEF); author of *CrossTalk: Where Life & Scripture Meet*

"Just when you thought you had read all the good books about love, and many not so good ones, along comes William Smith's *Loving Well*. It is marvelous—full of biblical insight and practical wisdom. It guides the reader through numerous real-life challenges and provides poignant and gracious solutions to them. I commend it with enthusiasm!"

Dr. William Edgar, DrThéol, Professor of Apologetics, Westminster Theological Seminary; author of *Truth in All Its Glory*

"This wonderful book by a seasoned pastor and Christian counselor provides practical, Christ-centered guidance for growing authentic, vulnerable, and loving relationships. I highly recommend this book."

Philip G. Monroe, PsyD, Professor of Counseling & Psychology; Director, MA Counseling Program, Biblical Seminary, Hatfield, PA

"Bill Smith knows Jesus, knows people, and brings them together in this practical, inviting treatment of Jesus' love for us. This book will help you, in detailed ways, to know Jesus better and to convey his love to others."

Robert D. Jones, Author; pastor; biblical counseling professor at Southeastern Seminary

"Whether it's that irritating neighbor down the street, the know-it-all at the office, the friend who misunderstands us, the person at church who drains us, children who don't give us the respect we think we deserve, or a spouse whom we disappoint and fail—this book addresses common roadblocks to loving and being a blessing to those God brings into our lives."

John Freeman, President, Harvest USA

"Dr. Bill Smith calls us to experience the beauty of true unconditional love from God through Christ and empowers his readers to break free from the lies we once believed to abounding, courageous love for those around us. If you long to live saturated in love that truly transforms you, this book is for you!"

Rev. Andrew Hudson, Lead Pastor, Chelten Baptist Church, PA

"*Loving Well* teaches us how to forgive, become authentically honest, show sympathy by renouncing our stingy demeanor, and reflect the kindness God has demonstrated to us. I hope these principles soak my crusty heart, and I love better because I have read it and practiced what I learned."

Dr. Penny Freeman, LPC, The Counseling Center at Chelten Baptist, PA

Loving Well

(Even If You Haven't Been)

WILLIAM P. SMITH

New
Growth
Press

New Growth Press, Greensboro, NC 27404
www.newgrowthpress.com

Cover Design: Brandon Hill Design, bhilldesign.com
Interior Design and Typesetting: North Market Street Graphics, Lancaster, PA

ISBN-13: 978-1-936768-29-5
ISBN-10: 1-936768-29-1

Library of Congress Cataloging-in-Publication Data

Smith, William P., 1965–
Loving well : (even if you haven't been) / William P. Smith.
   p. cm.
Includes bibliographical references (p. 253) and index.
ISBN-13: 978-1-936768-29-5 (alk. paper)
ISBN-10: 1-936768-29-1 (alk. paper)
1. Love—Religious aspects—Christianity. I. Title.
BV4639.S636 2012
241'.4—dc23   2011034484

Printed in the United States of America

19 18 17 16 15 14 13 12   1 2 3 4 5

To all those who have taught me so much
by gifting me with their love,
beginning with the One who loved me first.

Acknowledgments

Over the years, I've been privileged to live with slightly fewer than forty different people. That creates a hassle when an employer wants to run a background check, but it's been glorious when it comes to showing me the many facets of love.

Among those who have welcomed me not only into their homes, but also into their lives, are my family of origin (William and Birute Smith, Genie Barry, and Audra Stuart), all the members of the "Brotherhood," Scott and Gretchen Schwartzman, Brent Ellison, the guys from the West Philly ministry houses, John and Becca Hagerty, Bill and Lona DeHeer, along with my wife, Sally, and our three children: Cassie, Timmy, and Daniel. Thank you all for loving me and putting up with me.

Thank you also to the many people and places who invited me to try this material on their people: Redeemer Presbyterian Church of New Orleans, Louisiana; Oakland International Fellowship and Pittsburgh Chinese Church Oakland in western Pennsylvania; Bethel Baptist Church in Wilmington, Delaware; Harvey Cedars

Bible Conference on the coast in New Jersey; Perish No More in Lancaster, Pennsylvania; and the Community Evangelical Church in Elverson, Pennsylvania.

Thank you especially to Chelten Baptist Church in Dresher, Pennsylvania, for not only allowing me to test run some of the book, but also for encouraging me to make the time to put these thoughts down in written form. Extra thanks to my lead pastor and friend, Andy Hudson, who continues to believe that my writing adds to our ministry rather than takes me away from it. I love partnering with you, brother!

My thanks to another friend, Karen Teears, President of New Growth Press, who also continues to believe in me and work with me.

I am deeply grateful for the editorial input I received. My friends Fred and Jayne Bahrenberg gave extensive and encouraging feedback on an early draft. Sally Smith went the second mile literally as she worked through the manuscript twice.

As senior editor at New Growth Press, Barbara Juliani wore many hats, encouraging and challenging me as well as shepherding the project through its various stages.

I am deeply grateful to my editor, Jeff Gerke, who helped me rescue the good pieces of this book out of the mire I presented to him. He has that rare gift of being able to say "Your baby is ugly" without being offensive, while giving clear direction for what to do to improve it. Thanks too to Irene Stoops who cleaned up the final copy making it more readable. It goes without saying that the mistakes and bad decisions still in it are entirely my own.

This book belongs to all of you in a special way.

"By this all people will know that you are my disciples, if you have love for one another."

—Jesus

Contents

Escaping an Empty Way of Life

I stood outside, shivering in the cold, "talking" to God. *Venting* would be the more honest description. I had just thrown down the papers I was working on and stalked out of the room after unloading on one of my children, who had been repeatedly interrupting me every few minutes. My parting words were, "I am so frustrated right now. It doesn't matter what I say or do, you don't get it. It doesn't matter if I speak gently to you. It doesn't matter if I ignore you. It doesn't matter if I explode! You just keep coming. I don't know what to do with you."

I hate those times. I have no interest in verbally bashing my kids, making them feel like I'm never satisfied with them. And yet, I also don't want them to grow up believing that the world is all about them. What I'd just done wasn't terribly loving (I get that), but in that moment I didn't have any idea what else to do, so I ended up doing something that broke down the relationship instead of building it.

Ever been there? That place where, despite the fact that you really do want to love the people around you, somehow it all goes south? Either you do something to shred the friendship or you face something you don't know how to handle. You've tried everything you do know, and nothing seems to help. As a pastoral counselor, I have lots of friends who share those feelings.

Friends like Tasha and Maurice. Tasha is unhappy with her job and would really rather stay home with the baby, only they can't afford to have her do that. So every time she comes home, she complains to Maurice about how bad work was.

Maurice, however, doesn't know what to do with her complaints. His preferred role of being the funny, lighthearted guy just doesn't seem to work like it used to with her. So he prefers to switch on the TV during dinner and watch it into the night, or play card games with her, or do some other activity that safely insulates him from an intimidating conversation.

She likes him, but feels alone and abandoned. So guess what she does about her loneliness? She complains about it, adding it to the complaints about her job. And when she complains, he feels more helpless and confused, so he finds new ways to ignore her. And 'round and 'round they go. You wouldn't say he's a bad man or she's a miserable woman, but they don't know how to engage each other in a helpful way.

Most of the time, my friends and I don't set out trying to hurt anyone, especially those we really care about. We're relational creatures, made in the image of the great communal, three-in-one God. We long for relationships. Intentionally undermining our closest relationships would be counterproductive to our whole nature and desire. And yet we do just that. We watch them slip through our fingers—or worse, we see ourselves actively poisoning them simply by doing what feels right in the moment.

Because you've picked up this book, you probably know what broken relationships feel like. You see yourself damaging your closest friendships or not knowing how to bring healing when someone else harms them. Sometimes these unhealthy patterns and reactions can feel so natural that you don't even think about how they came about. You might not even realize how many of them you've adopted from other people. You may only be aware that, in the moment, the strategy seems to get you what you want.

Patrice pulls away from situations she doesn't like by withdrawing from people and refusing to talk to them. Her reaction makes complete sense when you learn that for her whole life she witnessed her father controlling her mother with the silent treatment. You probably wouldn't be too surprised to discover that this was the example he had while growing up in *his* home. Each generation learned how to relate to others from the generation before, even if those ways soured the closest relationships they had.

We are all fully responsible for the ways we mistreat each other, *and* we have all learned from the bad examples we've had. Nature (your own sinful inclinations) and nurture (the things you've experienced from others) join forces to undermine your relationships. They produce what the apostle Peter refers to as "the empty way of life handed down to you from your forefathers" (1 Peter 1:18, NIV).

Some people have more "empty way of life" quotient than others, but every person has embraced a legacy of emptiness—patterns of relating that seem right in the moment, but that ultimately tear friendships apart. These patterns are truly insane. What else can you call it when you repeatedly engage your children, spouse, parents, or friends in the same destructive ways even though you realize you're driving them away?

For someone like Patrice, the empty ways she deals with are primarily identified by the ongoing presence of evil. People in those positions experienced an aggressive negative relational style and had to react to it. Some become comfortable adopting the model as their own by taking the junkyard dog approach. They relate to others with the belief that, "If what wins arguments and protects me in this family is being loud, sarcastic, or insulting, then I will be the loudest, meanest, most caustic person in the room!" Others who have no interest in competing at that level develop self-protective strategies that keep everyone else at arm's length.

Empty ways of life, however, are not always defined by the active presence of evil. Just as often they are characterized by the *absence* of positive elements that would foster healthy relationships.

Nick's wife noted that his parents essentially ignored him after providing for his physical needs. Robert's family was more extreme. He didn't know what a hug felt like growing up. No one touched in his family nor wanted to. They didn't own a couch, only a collection of individual chairs. Walking through his living room daily reinforced the relational message "you are on your own in this life." That lack of physical connection mirrored the lack of intimacy at all other levels. Little wonder that these men struggled to know how to connect with their wives and kids.

Other families are not as dramatic in their dysfunction but still leave out many crucial relational elements. Some people never heard a parent say "I'm sorry; please forgive me." Others don't know what it is to hear "I love you. I'm proud of you. I'm so glad to see you!" Still others didn't experience someone pursuing them, inviting them back to relationship when they'd strayed, or simply affirming their feeling that life isn't very nice sometimes.

Without experiencing a healthy way of relating in your life, it's really hard to know it's even missing, much less that it's an essential element to give someone else. The absence of positive relational interactions gets passed on just as surely as the presence of negative patterns.

Spend just a little bit of time with God's people and you'll quickly learn that empty ways of life abound even in the middle of the redeemed community. Small home fellowship groups don't know how to embrace the quirky single guy who comes for a few weeks, so he quietly drops off the radar. Warring factions break out in the congregation over what style of music we sing or how we decorate the building. Elders approach their congregation with a heavy hand or back way off with no hand. Leaders fail, like they have all the way back to Noah, and no one knows how to put Humpty Dumpty together again.

People are lured into church by hearing the language of intimacy, authenticity, and genuineness, but when they experience their absence, they are left feeling even more hurt than before. They had hoped finally to find a safe place where they could experience being loved, only to realize that Christians are not really all that good at it. Instead of being welcomed and embraced, often they can end up isolated and alone. So they walk away discouraged and cynical—with good reason.

Does any of this resonate with your own experience? Over the past twenty-five years of professional and volunteer ministry, I have yet to meet the person who doesn't struggle at some point in his or her relationships.

Maybe you find yourself undermining the relationships that are most important to you. Or maybe someone else is hurting you and you don't know how to invite that person to something better. Or maybe you just find your relationships stagnate and don't grow richer.

If that's you, you're not alone. *And* you don't have to settle for these empty ways of life. You can exchange those patterns for others that promote deep unity and peacefulness—patterns that offer a satisfying and rich relationship to the people around you.

In short, you can learn to love well.

Jesus Loves Us Out of Emptiness

Peter draws our attention to the empty ways of life only in order to highlight that we have been redeemed from them by the precious blood of Christ (1 Peter 1:18–19). God cares about the hold these destructive patterns have on you, and he made a way to free you from them. They don't have to control how you live and react in your relationships.

Now you may expect me to fill the rest of this book with lists of helpful hints and biblical principles for maximizing the positive things and minimizing the negatives in your relationships. But escaping an empty way of life does not rely on principles—it relies on a person. And not just a person who comes and does things *for* you or is an example *outside of* you, but a person who comes and relates *to* you.

I'm afraid that too many times we hold up Jesus as though he were simply a model of brilliant living—one who would inspire us to live a holy life in the same way that we extol the virtues of George Washington, Abraham Lincoln, Mahatma Gandhi, and Mother Teresa. The problem with that thinking is that models alone are unable to make you want to follow their example. They point out the way for you to go, but they don't empower you to walk down that path. They might inspire you, but inspiration alone is not enough to actually move you.

Over the years I have heard a number of great stories of people who have done amazing things or overcome incredible obstacles—a father who enters marathons, pushing his wheelchair-bound son; a married couple who adopts 19 children with special needs over the course of their lifetime; or the concert musician who plays at Carnegie Hall because of the countless hours of practice she spent with her instrument. Those examples are stirring. Inwardly I cheer for those people and wish them the best.

Though I am inspired by their stories, however, my own lifestyle has not changed in the least. It takes far more than inspiration to escape an empty way of life. I've not yet been driven by these examples to take up jogging, adopt even one child, or pick up an instrument. They truly are praiseworthy examples, but they're outside of me. Therefore, by themselves, they are insufficient to move me.

Jesus is different. His examples of loving and serving are not things that happen outside of me–things I dispassionately observe. Far from being an uninvolved spectator to his reconciling work, I'm a recipient of his gracious actions. He *is* my example, but he is also my experience. In experiencing him, I not only develop a personal sense of what he calls me to, but I also gain the power to live out that calling with others.

God understands that you don't always know how to love people, so he does not insist you figure out how to bootstrap yourself into relationships. Instead, he makes sure you already know exactly what love is before he requires you to love others. As the apostle John put it, "In this is love, not that we have loved God, but that he loved us . . . if God so loved us, we also ought to love one another" (1 John 4:10–11, in larger context of vv. 7–21). It's only after having been loved that you respond with love. You love him back, and you reach out to share with others a tiny portion of the love that you yourself have received.

> *It's only after having been loved that you respond with love. You love him back, and you reach out to share with others a tiny portion of the love that you yourself have received.*

In my relationship with God, what's always been most important is the quality of his love for me, not the quality of my love for him. It's only as the reality of his love becomes my present experience that I will be more concerned about expressing my love to others than insisting they express theirs for me.

Too often I get this order backward with my children, like when I blew up at my child earlier. Those are the days when I keep careful track of all the ways it seems they don't care nearly enough about me. I become consumed with how they don't consider the pressures of my schedule when they want me to chauffeur them to their next sports game or to the store. I grumble about how they don't respect my property as they trample through the garden or slam the doorknob through the drywall. And I fume over how they're more interested in my money than my friendship. I confess, I have a hard time being greeted at the door after a long, hard day with "Hi, Daddy—can I have my allowance?"

In those moments, I get caught believing that what most needs to change in my family is them. They need to be more considerate, more respectful, and more grateful. In other words, I wrongly believe that our relationship is dependent on the quality of their love for me.

That's backward from the way I experience Jesus. The way he treats me, both historically and in the present, gives me the experience of being loved. And it is that experience that allows me to respond to him and extend myself to others, which is the real need of the people I live with. My family needs me to pursue them like Jesus pursues me. They need me to forgive them like Jesus forgives me. They need me to like them, engage with them, and share myself with them just as Jesus likes me, engages with me, and shares himself with me.

And that's where there is a disconnect for many people. They don't have a sense of the risen Christ relating to them in real time in a helpful, positive way. Whether I'm serving in my home church or traveling to others, I regularly interact with people who can explain historically what Jesus has done for them and who genuinely look forward to what he will do in eternity. But his present activities in their lives remain a cloudy mystery.

In turn, they struggle to communicate love to others in any tangible, recognizable form. This recognition forms the working thesis of this book: only through a present, rich, practical relationship with Jesus will you be able to develop rich, practical relationships with each other.

Your Human Relationships Flow from the God You Worship

The way I live out my relationships with people is one of the clearest indicators of how healthy my relationship with the Lord is. If I live knowing that God moves toward me all day long and invites me to move toward him, then I will engage people positively in their lives. But if I wait for others to give themselves to me first, then I show that I really don't believe or regularly experience this

> The way I live out my relationships with people is one of the clearest indicators of how healthy my relationship with the Lord is.

God who is reconciling people to himself. Either way, I live out the truth that you become whatever you worship.

Sadly, there are so many bad gods waiting to take Jesus' place. There's the false notion of God as a deity who sits in heaven, vaguely interested in your life, but who keeps himself pretty detached and aloof. Or there's the god who is only disengaged until you do something wrong. Then he springs into action, pulling out a long list of your failures and threatening you if you don't shape up. Or worse, maybe you've found the god who smiles at you a lot, but is too weak to challenge you or help you when you need it. The hard reality is that if your god is distant, critical, scary, or impotent then you will mimic that quality about him in the ways you treat those around you.

Thank God he doesn't leave you to those gods. Jesus came to redeem you from living out those empty ways of life handed down to you by your forefathers.

Throughout Scripture you see one overarching storyline: a good Father welcomes homeless orphans into his family by searching for them, rescuing them, embracing them, providing for them, and nurturing them. With that experience of life, you now have reason to hope for something different in the way you live with others. And hope is exactly what I need every day of my life.

My kids and I had a really rough week that felt like every interaction turned into a half-hour argument that I didn't handle very well. As the week wore on I became increasingly out of control, and I responded more harshly and critically each time. It was not a good week. Ironically, a few days later I was scheduled to give a radio interview for a booklet I had written entitled *How Do I Stop Losing It with My Kids?* I felt like such a hypocrite. I reread the booklet and kept thinking, *Hmm, that's a good idea. I wonder who wrote that?* Or, *Oh! Wish I had remembered to try that.*

At the end of the program, the interviewer asked one final question. He said, "Okay, this has been helpful, but what about the person who *has been* losing it—maybe for years? Who has been failing over and over again? What hope does that person have?"

I replied, "Well, honestly, that's me this morning. And my hope is that not only am I a parent in my family, but I'm also a child in a better family with a much better Father. And my Father is absolutely committed to being involved in my life, parenting me so that I can be the parent that he always meant me to be."

I need that hope. And I need even more than hope. It's easy to say we need to love others well, but that statement can feel pretty vague when I face a particular challenge with caring for a real, flesh-and-blood person in the smaller, practical moments of life. For instance, what does loving others well look like when I need to restore a relationship that I just damaged? At times like that, I need to know *specifically* what love looks like.

Dazzling Love

I find it helpful to think of love as a large jewel with many facets. Each facet gives you a glimpse into the jewel's essence because each is part of the same jewel. But every viewpoint has a sparkle and radiance all its own.

Throughout this book we're going to investigate fifteen facets of *the love we experience from God* because it is in these ways that he invites you to mature as you relate to other people with love. While there are many more that we could explore—and we will as eternity unwinds—these fifteen form a solid toolkit that, as you grow in them, will affect the quality of relationships you currently have.

You can love other people only out of your own experience of being loved. Or, to say it in reverse, you cannot pass along what you yourself have not received. Does that sound limiting to you or maybe even completely demoralizing? Like you're fated never to rise above the inadequacies other people have passed down to you?

That's where a relationship with Jesus is intensely practical. Because you are his, you are not beyond hope—nor are your relationships. Missing out on being loved well by other humans does not doom your present relationships. In your present, ongoing relationship with Jesus, you can receive from him all the love you need to give to others.

He can give you what you never received, and then you can pass it to those around you who need it.

We'll approach our topic in three parts. In Part I, "Love That Responds to a Broken World," we'll look at those aspects of love that help you move toward your friend as she experiences sin or suffering so that she knows she is not alone.

Part II, "Love That Reaches Out to Build Others Up," focuses on aspects of love that show someone else you're more interested in helping him be all God ever meant him to be, than using him to make yourself feel good.

And in Part III, "Love That Enjoys Heaven Now," we'll look at the kinds of love that allow people to see and trust your heart for them so that you can enjoy being together now.

Let me offer one caveat before we dive in: please be careful not to fall into a mindset that looks for quick, immediate results when you reach out to love well. Learning these fifteen aspects *will* improve the overall tone of your relationships, but they are not part of a guaranteed formula that works like this: if you do _____, then everyone else will respond to you with _____. Rather, you can expect to receive these elements from Jesus, and as you practice them you will find yourself moving in harmony with the way he runs his world rather than against it. In that sense your life will be better, you will be more satisfied, and your relationships will change for the better.

As a friend, lay leader, counselor, seminary professor, conference speaker, and pastor I have seen many people turn away from destructive patterns and enter into the freedom of healthy relationships. That's been quite a privilege. Beyond all those instances of seeing people love well, however, I'm most encouraged to believe you really can escape your empty ways of living because of the way relationships in my own home have grown healthier over the years.

Remember that I told you how hard my child and I worked to ruin our relationship? Sadly, there are still plenty of times when we collectively rip at the fabric of our relationship. That's the product of real people in a really fallen world. But even more significant is what we do with those destructive moments. By God's kindness, we continue to learn how to repair the rips we create and celebrate the greater number of times when we move closer without damaging our friendship.

That's the product of being loved by a gracious God in a grace-infused world. If Jesus can help free me and my family from being stuck in bad patterns, and teach us to create beneficial ones, then I know he can help you too.

As you are introduced to each way he loves us, I think you'll be surprised by how intimately involved God is with you. I know I have been surprised. After seeing and re-experiencing him in new ways, I suspect you'll hardly be able to wait to give that experience to someone else!

PART I

LOVE THAT RESPONDS TO A BROKEN WORLD

On this planet you face the reality of sin and suffering, especially in your relationships. That's a given. How you respond to others in a fallen world, however, makes all the difference. Your reactions either compound those struggles or bring relief. Two common approaches—retreating from hardships or lashing out during them—only produce greater problems down the road.

Jesus never took those paths. He never lost his friendship with God through his struggles. Even though his life was not easy, it was good. More than that, his response to those hardships actually cemented his relationships with his friends. They grew in their love for him and for each other, which set the stage for you to taste his goodness as well.

As Jesus moves toward you, he teaches you how to move toward others—toward the suffering, hurting people around you—rather than driving them away.

In Part I we're going to explore several ways of responding to someone's experience of brokenness in a way that says to her, "You are not alone. I am in this with you." By learning to share your presence with someone else, you will lessen the pain and difficulty of that struggle for her, rather than increasing the damage inflicted by sin or suffering.

Chapters in Part I:

1. Comforting Love: Running to Those Who Are Suffering

2. Sympathetic Love: Taking on Each Other's Sorrows

3. Struggling Love: Confessing Our Temptations to Each Other

4. Forgiving Love: Covering a Multitude of Sins

5. Longsuffering Love: Patiently Bearing with Each Other

CHAPTER I

Comforting Love: Running to Those Who Are Suffering

The first aspect of God's love we will explore is how he moves toward you when you suffer. That simple act of coming near to share himself in your difficult moments eases your sufferings because you learn that you are not alone. It sounds simple, but in the face of someone's pain, that thought is hard to remember and even harder to do. If you are going to become someone who loves others well when they suffer, you will first have to see how God comes near to you in your misery.

It's Easy to Run from Suffering

Ray pastors a church in New Orleans. He never tires of reminding me that God makes his home among the suffering. I went to visit him two and a half years after Hurricane Katrina had devastated the city. At that time, the storm had become part of vaguely remembered history for much of the rest of the country. The only remnant most of us still encountered were fuel prices that hadn't fallen back to pre-Katrina levels. But for those living in New Orleans, the storm was not part of their past; it was something they lived with every day.

While most of the loose debris had been removed, other reminders of the storm were everywhere you looked. Boarded-up commercial buildings had not been repaired and didn't look likely to ever be repaired. Tap water was still not quite safe to drink. FEMA trailers, designed for a maximum of one-year occupancy, were still being used as we drove past mile after mile of empty, condemned homes. To put this into hard numbers, Ray pointed out that if the 520 licensed contractors in the city each were to completely restore 10 houses a year, it would take another 35 years to rebuild the city.

The most ominous reminder, however, was a dull yellow-brown stripe that ran horizontally across buildings, bridges, and every other permanent structure. This line marked the high-water stage of the flood. As the water slowly evaporated under the sweltering September heat, it left a six-to-eight-inch-wide sediment stripe across everything it touched. It's an eerie reminder of the scale of what happened when you drive along the road or walk along a street and calculate how far below the surface of the water you would have been—four feet, eight feet, ten feet, or more.

Signs of pain and suffering are everywhere. They are daily reminders that all is not right, that life is hard. Without being overly dramatic, let me say that suffering formed the context for every interaction that people had in that city. And that reality overwhelms people and burns them out.

The year before I visited, 120 people became members at Ray's church . . . while 60 members left the area. It is not an easy calling. But among the people who remained, I didn't sense that pessimism was the reigning emotion. Rather, they shared a sense of God's special presence among them.

That is the kind of comforting presence you and I need as well.

Suffering is not unique to a few people who have chosen to remain in a flood-ravaged city. Rather, after humanity's fall into sin, suffering became as common to us as the air we breathe. Spend a little time talking to people and you will hear a repeated theme of suffering in everyone's story.

If you live on this planet, you cannot escape suffering. Some people cause their own suffering by the choices that they make—and so they reap the consequences of their sin. Others seem to fall into suffering through no fault of their own, as with chronic illnesses or things that happen to them unexpectedly. In either case, suffering is so prevalent that you rub shoulders with it daily in your own life and in the lives of the people around you.

Sadly, many of our responses are inadequate to this great and unending need. Some of us grow desensitized. We become so used to seeing suffering and pain that we tune it out. Worse, we grow calloused, getting to the point where people's hardships don't affect us.

Or, if we don't lose our sensitivity, we become fatigued. We get discouraged. We don't know what to do or how to handle the overload because it is always present, and so we wear out. Then we pull back, retreating inside our own worlds, reducing contact with others to protect ourselves.

In either case, the result is the same; we remove ourselves from the people who need us the most. Maybe you know what that is like. You realize that part of the reason there's now distance between you and your spouse or friend is because there seems no end to his needs. These responses are very understandable. They're very human.

Thankfully, God is very different.

Jesus, Our Sorrow Carrier

We all know that Jesus carried our sins on the cross, but have you let yourself think much about how he also carried our sorrows?[1]

Isaiah the prophet describes the Messiah who is to come in chapter 53 of his book. Look at verses 2–4:

> He had no form or majesty that we should look at him,
> and no beauty that we should desire him.
> He was despised and rejected by men;
> a man of sorrows, and acquainted with grief;
> and as one from whom men hide their faces
> he was despised, and we esteemed him not.
> Surely he has borne our griefs
> and carried our sorrows;
> yet we esteemed him stricken,
> smitten by God, and afflicted.

Life on earth was just not fun for Jesus. Do you know what it is to be despised? To be rejected? To have people treat you with contempt? Jesus knew it all. "Despised and rejected" is not a vague, theological concept. It has a face and a voice.

"He had no form or majesty that we should look at him and no beauty that we should desire him," Isaiah says. There was nothing impressive about Jesus. Nothing about him physically that would draw others to him. At best, people overlooked him. But people aren't always at their best. "Despised and rejected" implies that he attracted negative attention and ridicule. Know how that feels?

Can you hear people making comments about his mother—how her pregnancy with him showed she must have been sleeping around before she got married? Did the brothers he grew up with say anything to him about not sharing the same dad? Despised and rejected.

Did people think he was too religious for his own good—that a little religion was a good thing, but that he went overboard?

His mother and brothers showed up wanting to see him one time when he was teaching (Matthew 12:46; Luke 8:19). That sounds positive, doesn't it? It takes on a darker cast, however, when you read how Mark records it in chapter 3 of his book. There we learn that they wanted to see him so they could forcibly take him away because they believed he was out of his mind (v. 21). Despised and rejected.

This was a man of sorrows who was acquainted with grief. He knew intimately what sorrow and sadness were. He lived in the land of grief. But against all our modern psychological expectations, his experiences didn't turn him sour. He didn't become bitter or sociopathic. Instead, he moved to help those who also lived in the land of sadness—he bore *our* griefs and carried *our* sorrows. Not only did he have his own unhappy experiences to bear, he reached out and burdened himself with the sadness that other people carried.

When we think of the cross and what Jesus did there, we rightly focus on how he paid the penalty for our sins so that we could be friends with God. But he did more. According to Isaiah, he was also weighed down with the things we suffer in this life. Not only did he experience carrying our sins, but also the consequences that our sins and the sins of others leave us with. He bore our sins *and* our sorrows.

And we didn't cheer him on or appreciate him for his sacrifice. No, "we esteemed him stricken, smitten by God, and afflicted." We thought he was cursed by God even while he was experiencing our world, carrying our sins. He left all the comforts he had in heaven to enter our world to know us and rescue us and make our burdens lighter, and we thought he was a loser.

But he didn't care. Instead, we see him almost running toward suffering people to help them. Blind men, lepers, paralytics, the hungry, the fearful, and the scared all found relief as he entered their worlds. He put things right for them. But most importantly, he shared himself—he touched them, talked to them, and wept with them. In sharing himself, by being present with them in their sorrows, he eased their suffering.

You and I can do that too. We can be present in the sorrows of our loved ones.

When Amy risked letting her friends know that her unwed daughter was pregnant, Kathy dropped everything she was doing and raced over to Amy's house—because you cannot phone in the hug she needed. Kathy learned that truth from Jesus, who had often shared himself with her in her dark moments.

This doesn't take specialized training or a professional degree. You only need to practice being aware that people who are struggling need your physical presence.

Together in the Hard Places

Surprisingly, we also see Jesus looking for this kind of love to come alongside and comfort him in his sorrows. After sharing the Passover meal with his disciples on the night he was betrayed, he went into a garden.

> And they went to a place called Gethsemane. And he said to his disciples, "Sit here while I pray." And *he took with him* Peter and James and John, and began to be greatly distressed and troubled. (Mark 14:32–33, emphasis added)

He was facing the most challenging moment of his life. He was about to enter suffering that goes beyond description, and he needed to connect with his Father. And yet, that isn't all he wanted; he also wanted his human friends to enter into that difficult moment with him. What did he expect they would do for him? There wasn't anything they could do . . . except be there with him, watching and praying.

Part of comforting love involves human presence—not just divine presence—and even Jesus wanted that. But Jesus not only wanted it, he invited it.

Does that surprise you? Many people believe that all you need is the Bible and Jesus to get through life. And so we discount the need to be in each other's lives as we go through hard times.

> *Part of comforting love involves human presence— not just divine presence*

Kimberly had been wrestling with the fear of having someone close to her die. She'd lost two children and was scared of losing her husband. That was a heavy weight to carry around. She was finally willing to admit it, and when she did she felt a huge sense of relief.

When I offered to help her work through why she was having so much trouble trusting the Lord, she jumped at the opportunity and expressed how happy she was for the chance. Simply making the time to be with her meant a lot. But then I didn't see or hear from her again. Several weeks later I learned that someone else had talked to her. This person had told her, "Oh, your problem is that you just need to have more faith. You would be fine if you could just connect with God a little bit more or a little bit better."

Funny how the Son of God didn't believe that. Jesus actively sought out human companionship at the time of his greatest need. Almost sounds blasphemous, doesn't it? He didn't think that all he needed was God, *nor* did he think all he needed was human community. He longed for both to give him comfort, just as he had offered his presence to others to comfort them.

There is something vitally important about being with each other as we're going through the hard places in our lives.

Move toward the Suffering

Suffering isolates. No two experiences of suffering are exactly the same, which leaves you thinking, "No one else will be able to understand this." So you tend to shut yourself off from others. That sense of isolation only increases when others leave you alone.

Somehow, amid all the prenatal checkups and ultrasounds, the doctors missed that Maggie's baby suffered a rare congenital defect, a reality that finally became evident during her emergency C-section. There was nothing anyone could do for the little one, so Maggie and her husband took him home and cared for him until he died three weeks later.

Can you imagine what that was like? She had carried him to full term, dreamed of what he might look like, started building hopes for him, gotten everything together to take care of him . . . and then he wasn't there anymore. Her church family rallied around her and her family—initially. But then, slowly, they stopped asking how she was. Who knew what she might say? And so, although they didn't intend to, they effectively ignored what she was going through. Three months later, to them it was as though nothing had happened. They continued as if things were normal.

For her, things were anything but normal. Her world had been turned upside down. She was distressed in her body, her emotions, and her immediate family. She was still grieving and would be for a long time. But without someone moving toward her, the option for her to grieve with others was not open to her. She needed people to continue moving toward her, to break through the barriers that kept her alone with her grief.

Suffering doesn't have a lifespan you can conveniently schedule or contain. There are no easy, three-step ways of moving through it or predicting it. That's why Jesus' solution is personal. He urges you to move toward suffering people because that's what you've experienced from him.

Sharing the Comfort God Gave You

Thankfully, the early church understood how necessary it was for them to actively comfort each other. Listen to how Paul begins his second letter to his friends in the city of Corinth:

> Blessed be the God and Father of our Lord Jesus Christ, the Father of mercies and God of all comfort, who comforts us in all our affliction, so that we may be able to comfort those who are in any affliction, with the comfort with which we ourselves are comforted by God. For as we share abundantly in Christ's sufferings, so through Christ we share abundantly in comfort too. If we are afflicted, it is for your comfort and salvation; and if we are comforted, it is for your comfort, which you experience when you patiently endure the same sufferings that we suffer. Our hope for you is unshaken, for we know that as you share in our sufferings, you will also share in our comfort.
>
> For we do not want you to be ignorant, brothers, of the affliction we experienced in Asia. For we were so utterly burdened beyond our strength that we despaired of life itself. Indeed, we felt that we had received the sentence of death. But that was to make us rely not on ourselves but on God who raises the dead. He delivered us from such a deadly peril, and he will deliver us. On him we have set our hope that he will deliver us again. You also must help us by prayer, so that many will give thanks on our behalf for the blessing granted us through the prayers of many. (2 Corinthians 1:3–11)

Pay attention to the event that forms the context for this letter. Paul alludes to it in the second paragraph. What he and his companions were going through was so bad that it was more than they could take. They felt so strongly that the sentence of death had been served upon them that they stopped hoping they would survive. They knew very clearly that they were about to die.

Perhaps you know what that experience is like. You've been told by the doctor that you have a life-threatening cancer. You've watched helplessly as another car plowed through an intersection and slammed into yours. You've been in an accident at home or on the job that you were powerless to prevent and that you knew could easily kill you. Paul said he knew what it was like to know deep down that his life was over.

Yet even in that experience Paul had a sense that he wasn't alone. He knew God was involved, using this experience to teach him not to rely on himself but on God, who raises the dead. Many of us would have balked at that point. We would have said that if there was any purpose involved, then it would have been to rely on God to keep us from dying. Paul knew God's involvement didn't always mean he would remain safe.

God's presence guarded his life this time, but even more than that, it comforted him through the experience. As surprising as you might find Paul's confidence—that it was in a God who raises the dead versus a God who keeps us from dying—his understanding of God's comfort is even more unexpected.

As you unpack his logic above, you realize that Paul believed the purpose of being comforted by God was so that he could give that experience away to someone else. God is the "God of all comfort, who comforts us in all our affliction, so that we may be able to comfort those who are in any affliction, with the comfort with which we ourselves are comforted by God" (2 Corinthians 1:3–4). In effect, he says to the Corinthians, "I didn't go through that experience for my benefit only (that is, so that I could learn to rely more on God), but so that *you* would be comforted through it."

Do you have any experiences like that? Times when you have gone through hardship but found comfort and grace through it, comfort that in some ways was even more meaningful for the people with whom you shared it?

My youngest son tends to pass out when he sees blood. He came in from playing in the snow one day, crying hard. He had been pushing his brother on a sled when the sled hit the porch deck and stopped. He, on the other hand, did not stop. His head kept going and smashed into the sled. He thought he had knocked a tooth out, given all the blood he saw. As he was tearfully telling us this, his eyes rolled up into his head and his body fell limp.

Once we brought him around we *really* needed to comfort him, so I began telling him there are a lot of people who have the same reaction to blood that he does—including myself. A number of years ago I finally stopped donating blood because I got tired of having to be revived. (I don't think the nurses enjoyed those experiences much either.)

It comforted my son to hear those stories of how I'd learned to live with the body and mind God had given me. As I shared them with him, he realized that he was not alone in his experience. He lives among fellow sufferers who can share some of his burden.

> *This is how we love: we share the stories of things we've faced. We don't do so to take center stage, but to communicate to someone else, "You're not weird. You belong."*

This is how we love: we share the stories of things we've faced. We don't do so to take center stage, but to communicate to someone else, "You're not weird. You belong."

Paul explains the reason this way:

> But God has so composed the body, giving greater honor to the part that lacked it, that there may be no division in the body, but that the members may have the same care for one another. If one member suffers, all suffer together; if one member is honored, all rejoice together. (1 Corinthians 12:24–26)

We are all part of the same body. Paul argues in Ephesians that while we are saved *as* individuals, we are saved *into* a community—a community that is modeled on our God and works together to display an image of him to a watching world. After all, God is a "community" composed of three distinct, fully divine persons, yet so intertwined and close that he calls himself one God. Our human community, bound together in the Holy Spirit, is also made up of many different persons, yet we collectively form one body—in the same way that I am composed of billions of individual cells, yet they all cohere in one person.

If *any* part of Christ's body hurts, then the whole body hurts, and it is only right that we would gather around that hurting part in order to care for him or her. If we didn't, we would be demonstrating a body that is unhealthy and sick. A simple but important part of love is to run to sufferers and share with them our presence and the comfort we ourselves have received.

Pause for a moment and think: who are the people you know who need the comfort of your presence in their suffering? Are there stories from your life that will comfort them?

That's what you see Paul doing in his relationships. He tells his story of suffering and finding God in the middle of it, in order to use that experience to help the people around him. While Jesus asked for companionship in his sufferings, Paul demonstrates how to be a companion for the suffering, how to share comfort with each other when we're hurting. God cares about our sufferings and can't stand to leave us alone in them. It is one of the primary attributes of his love.

Because we have experienced that kind of love from God, we find we can come alongside others to help relieve their suffering.

Being Present with the Suffering

When your child cries, you drop everything and go to her, don't you? Why? You want to see what's wrong. You want to help if you can. And especially, you want to comfort with your presence. Simply being there with her is comforting. The same is true of all your other relationships. People will know you love them when you prioritize being with them in their distress.

Ethan told me once of getting a phone call in which he learned that his son had been rushed to the emergency room. When he arrived at the hospital he was surprised, to say the least, to find that that his pastor was already there with his son. Surprised, but deeply touched. Think about that: the pastor was not a doctor, and he had no medical knowledge that could help the boy. But his rushing to be with the family was so important to them that I heard the story many years later.

As Stan, our Pastor of Compassion Ministries, toured my neighborhood following severe damage by strong winds, he explained to me, "When something like this happens, you go. You don't make a phone call." He understood what Jesus and Paul knew: personal contact during suffering, even if you have nothing to say, is one of the most special gifts you can offer.

> *... personal contact during suffering, even if you have nothing to say, is one of the most special gifts you can offer.*

Very likely, God is not calling you to relocate halfway across the country to a hurricane-plagued city set on the rim of the Gulf of Mexico (although if he is, I know a church that would warmly welcome you). But he is calling you to look around where you live and run to embrace those who are suffering.

Are there sufferers in your home? A child who's out of sorts today who needs you to realize that something at school went wrong? A

neighbor or friend at church who's been laid off, fallen ill, or tar-
geted by a cruel employer struggling to make ends meet? Having
seen their misery and having allowed it to touch you, you need to
move toward them so that they know they're not alone.

That's what Jesus does for you.

On Your Own

1. What surprises you as you meditate on how Jesus responds to
    suffering—both to his own and to other people's? What strikes
    you as you reflect on the interplay of relationship, comfort, and
    suffering within God's family?

2. Remind yourself of a time when you experienced the comfort
    of God. How would you describe it? Were you also comforted
    by other Christians at that time? In what ways were the experi-
    ences similar? Different?

3. Ask a few friends to share their own experiences of being com-
    forted by Jesus. What do they help you realize about the kind
    of comfort that God provides? What did you learn that would
    help you as you seek to be an agent of comfort in the lives of
    others?

4. During the past month, where have you reached out to comfort
    others with the comfort you have received? Who needs to re-
    ceive that from you now?

CHAPTER 2

Sympathetic Love: Taking on Each Other's Sorrows

In this chapter we will see what you do once you've moved toward someone in pain: you *sympathize* with him. That's another aspect of how God has loved you. He not only notices your pain, but he feels it so keenly that he identifies with you in it. He enters into your suffering, creating an even deeper bond with you by letting you know he understands what life is like for you.

You can extend that love to others by what you do when you are with hurting people—how you act, the attitude that you bring, the things you say, and especially the things you don't say. The closer those elements mirror the ways you've experienced Jesus coming to you, the more you will connect with people's hearts as they struggle.

Putting the Pain into Words

"I just came over to give you a hug," Robin said as she picked her way carefully over the cratered ruin of what had once been a beautiful shade garden.

Drooping plants, craving relief from the sun, were left exposed amid the deep gashes left by tree roots that had been pulled from the ground. In its 10-second visit to our neighborhood, the twister had claimed our triple-trunked, 100-foot sycamore, along with three other mature trees. I could barely hear Robin above the drone of the generator powering my refrigerator, but she spoke in a language that didn't need words and that went straight to my heart.

She, her husband, and their family had biked over to see us two days after the storm. The tears had been just behind my eyes most of the day. I'd spent long hours talking to people—caring friends, insurance adjusters, storm damage removal teams—but nothing had changed. The tree still filled the backyard, blocked my back door, barricaded the patio, crushed the garden, and stretched nearly across the entire width of the side street of our corner lot. It felt like a useless day. Topping it all off, I just couldn't stop thinking about how much time, energy, and money we'd spent on creating the garden that was now spoiled.

We'd never really gardened before, but a friend had convinced us to try. We'd gone to the nursery and selected scrawny green things that we were promised would grow into beautiful plants. Many didn't make it, but we persevered. We learned through trial and error, adding more plants and different ones until it was the nicest looking piece of our property. More than nice, it was beautiful. I loved looking at it. Walking around the garden after work was soothing. I'd sit on the patio or in the yard, just drinking in the colors and shapes. We enjoyed sharing it with others who came to visit.

Now, all that beauty was gone. I was sick at heart—and Robin knew it.

Not only did she get it, but her husband did as well. He spoke about all the hard work we'd invested and how it had paid off and how our present experience just plain hurt. His tender words and smile touched my heart. He forged a connection with me by putting my feelings into words. That's part of sympathy. It's one thing to have people ask how you're doing and invite you to talk about how you're feeling—it's quite another when someone expresses how you're feeling without you having to open your mouth. I knew he cared about how I felt because the things I couldn't find words for, he did, as we walked around the yard together. As they rode away, I felt lighter.

> It's one thing to have people ask how you're doing and invite you to talk about how you're feeling—it's quite another when someone expresses how you're feeling without you having to open your mouth.

Some days are like that. There are times when you serve and pour yourself out. And then there are days when you have nothing left to give, not even to yourself. Those are the days that teach you just how badly you need others in God's family. Robin and her family found me on *that* day. If you want to connect well with hurting people in your life, learn to grieve with them over what troubles them.

Very simply, my friends lived out the second half of God's command in Romans 12:15—"Rejoice with those who rejoice, weep with those who weep." The first part is easy and comes naturally. The second part is harder and not as much fun, but when they wept with me as I wept, it was life-giving.

Weep with Those Who Weep

Some people bristle at commands. They don't like to be told what to do, and they don't see the point of obeying. That's why we need to realize that God's commands are not arbitrary but are an extension of his character. They express who he is. Jesus tells us:

> "The good man brings good things out of the good stored up
> in his heart, and the evil man brings evil things out of the evil

stored up in his heart. For out of the overflow of his heart his mouth speaks" (Luke 6:45, NIV).

In other words, what you say expresses who you are on the inside. You speak in ways that show what you value and cherish. Your words reveal who you are.

The same is true of God. His words reveal his internal, invisible essence. So when he commands something, he's not merely telling you what to do, he's revealing what he himself is like. He's telling you what he values and what moves him.

Therefore, when he tells you to mourn with those who mourn, he's not making up rules because he has nothing better to do. He is not a cranky person who just loves bossing other people around. Nor is he merely concerned with organizing human societies in the best way possible as though we were a live version of a computer simulation game. Instead, his commands come from his heart and express who he is—what he feels, thinks, and believes in.

He has never had trouble weeping with people who weep. He loves people by letting them see how deeply moved he is by what breaks their hearts. Consider the story of Jesus' friend Lazarus.

Early in John 11 we learn that Lazarus was so sick that his sisters, Mary and Martha, asked Jesus to come heal him. But Jesus stayed where he was knowing that Lazarus would be dead before he set out to go see him. He even hinted that he was going to go anyway in order to raise him from the dead so that God might be glorified. Jesus already knew what he was going to find when he got to his friend, *and* he already knew what he was going to do. We pick up the story with Jesus having arrived at the town where Lazarus and his sisters had their home:

Now when Mary came to where Jesus was and saw him, she fell at his feet, saying to him, "Lord, if you had been here, my brother would not have died." When Jesus saw her weeping, and the Jews who had come with her also weeping, he was deeply moved in his spirit and greatly troubled. And he said, "Where have you laid him?" They said to him, "Lord, come and see." Jesus wept. So the Jews said, "See how he loved him!" But some of them said, "Could not he who opened the eyes of the blind man also have kept this man from dying?" (John 11:32–37)

Do you see all the ways Jesus is described? He was deeply moved in his spirit—that means he was profoundly touched inside himself. He was greatly troubled—also an internal thing. Something about what he was seeing was not okay with him. What that was is harder to understand. Was it the sorrow of his friends that troubled him? Or was it their lack of confidence that he could or would do something in the moment?

It's a bit ambiguous here, but it's clear that Jesus is not a stoic. He's affected by our lives. The way you act and respond to the difficulties of your life moves him. He is not hardened to your distress.

You see that even more clearly in the short, powerful verse 35: "Jesus wept." His weeping is tied directly to the comment, "See how much he loved him." Not only did he care about his friends, but he also let them see that he did. It was not okay with Jesus that Lazarus was dead. This was not merely an impersonal demonstration of power and glory. This was Jesus' friend, and he loved him deeply—so deeply that he cried.

But remember, he knew all this in advance, *and* he knew what he was going to do before he got there. He knew he was going to raise him from the dead and that he would be alive again. In just a few moments there would not be a dead man in front of him. There would only be his friend, restored to life. And yet he cried.

His absolute foreknowledge and omniscient power did not keep him from responding emotionally to what he experienced in the moment. He wept with those who wept.

So should we. Our friends need to see our tears over the broken parts of their lives. Part of love is letting them know that their pain matters deeply to us.

Weeping Over Not-Goodness

Jesus wholeheartedly embraced his humanity—dare I say, his divinity?—and wept over what had happened rather than exulting in what was about to happen. Giving God glory was worth waiting for and worth allowing Lazarus not to be healed. But Lazarus's death was not a good thing, so Jesus entered into that experience of not-goodness and wept.

I suspect that picture of your God makes sense to you. You're not surprised to see him weep because he is always among the suffering. His tears are an extension of his person. To paraphrase Joni Eareckson-Tada and Steve Estes, when suffering people open the Scriptures looking for comfort, they are never confronted by a verse that reads, "Jesus laughed."[1]

Sadly, there are probably times when someone has handled your struggles in a lighthearted way, hoping to "jolly you up." Or perhaps you've strained a relationship by taking someone else's pain too lightly. Do you know how revolting a thing it is when people are anything less than sober when you've experienced loss? It is an affront to your psyche. I wrestle with trying to find a way to express how dark and evil it is to ignore people's hurt when they're grieving. Let me see if a picture helps.

I have a friend who was in a horrible auto accident—his injuries were so extensive that the doctors put him into a drug-induced coma for ten days so he wouldn't feel the pain. After he came out of the coma they didn't tell him how badly others were hurt in the vehicle because they were afraid he would not have the strength to fight his way back to life. That meant he didn't learn for a number of weeks that others in the vehicle for whom he felt responsible had died . . . including his wife.

Imagine him, lying in the burn rehab, finally aware of the size of his loss, when in walked a "counselor" who was bubbly, chirpy, and cheerful.

This man has been to hell. He knows what it looks like and feels like, and he barely made it back. What did her mood convey to him? That life isn't so bad? That he should always look on the bright side of life? That losing his wife isn't that big a deal? That a little bit of time and effort will make him fine again? That he will have no problems?

My friend will carry around mental and physical memories all his life that were invalidated by the counselor's mood. She could not have communicated more clearly that she had no idea the depth of what he'd been through and was continuing to live out.

God is not like that. Nor can you be. Ignoring pain or changing the subject is neither helpful nor kind.

The pictures of God that you're given in Scripture show that he is touched by your grief. He weeps with those who weep. And in that simple, important act, you realize that he does understand. He is not insensitive. Your pain matters to him, and he's not okay with it. What you endure touches him.

This is part of the reason you are comforted by your God even when you realize he is sovereign over a world that is shot through with suffering. You realize that, as much as you don't understand your hurts, God is deeply touched by them. The longer you study how God has reacted to you in your own pain, the fewer times you will be calloused or indifferent to someone else's pain.

The Art of True Sympathy

God cares about how your sorrows, past and present, affect you. But he also cares about your future. Near the end of Scripture we are told, "He will wipe away every tear from their eyes" (Revelation 21:4).

That is such a tender expression of Jesus' heart for you. He knows you have cried, and it's not okay with him that you would cry for eternity. So he promises he will care for you in your weeping, removing anything that brings mourning or crying or pain.

More than that, by wiping your tears away, he shows you what to do for others. What a caring image: your God, stooping to smooth away the water tracks down your face. Is there a more intimate picture of what people do for each other when we grieve?

When was the last time you helped wipe away someone's tears?

There is so little I can do for my family when they cry. Even if I can fix what is broken, I cannot banish the pain of the breaking because that pain takes place inside the person. But I can hold them and smooth away tears. By doing that I let them know they are not alone. It says to them, "I'm here with you. And I'm not going anywhere. We will walk through this together." You will do that with another person only if you're touched by his tears. And you're more easily touched by someone else's tears when you know your God is touched by yours.

...you're more easily touched by someone else's tears when you know your God is touched by yours.

If you have been deeply hurt in your life, you may struggle to believe that your grief actually affects God. Or you may not fully agree that he bears your sorrows because they felt so heavy to you. Your sense of having had to carry the full weight of your burdens will keep you from longing to ease someone else's. If that's you, then take a look at this from Hebrews 4:[2]

Since then we have a great high priest who has passed through the heavens, Jesus, the Son of God, let us hold fast our confession. For we do not have a high priest who is unable to *sympathize* with our weaknesses, but one who in every respect has been tempted as we are, yet without sin. Let us then with confidence draw near to the throne of grace, that we may receive mercy and find grace to help in time of need. (Hebrews 4:14–16, emphasis added)

Sympathy is central to the meaning of this passage because true sympathy goes well beyond feeling bad for someone else. Real sympathy means to feel what they feel.[3] It's an insider's perspective of what it is like to be in the same position.

My daughter came down with a cold the night before the three kids and I were supposed to go to "Doughnuts with Dad" at their school. I told my oldest son, Timmy, that Cass would probably not go the next morning. He looked sad at this news, then said, "I wish I could just take her cold so that she could go and I'd wave goodbye to her in the morning." That's sympathy. It's caring so much about someone else that you would take his place in his pain if you could. It is the art of walking in someone else's shoes.

My third grade teacher, Mrs. Marston, however, was no such artist. She knew her subjects well, could teach them properly, and kept her classroom in order. But just as effectively she communicated that she had no sympathy for what it was like to be a kid.

I'm guessing she was in the vicinity of six feet tall and powerfully built. My elementary-school-age eyes remember her as taller than that, towering above us with not a hint of a smile. Her physical presence alone distanced her from us.

So did her approach to relationships. The time she came striding down the row and pounced on the book I was using to shield my toy from her was the last time I remember doing anything wrong in her class. It's also the only memory I have of that entire year. She wasn't abusive, but neither was she warm or inviting. She was not the person you moved toward to find help in your time of need.

Instead, she was the kind of person that you're convinced never was a child, but who sprang full grown like Athena from Zeus's head. She certainly didn't communicate that she had an inkling of what it was like to be a child—energetic, inquisitive, imaginative, and forced to sit for far too long through dull routines. I could not imagine going to her with a problem.

What a contrast she was to the lovely Miss Bowers, my second grade teacher. None of the boys would ever admit it, but I think most of us secretly had a crush on her from day one. In addition, her kindness only made us want to be good. One of her methods of dealing with misbehavior was to have everyone line up so she could "hug the badness" out of us.

Years later, when the Lord convicted me of having stolen something from her classroom, I wrote her an apology—in part because it was the right thing to do, but probably also because I suspected I would find grace and mercy. From the letter she wrote back, it was clear that I had. I have more and better memories of second grade. She was the kind of person you trusted when you were in trouble.

The people with whom you are in relationship need that too. They need the kind of love from you that says you can be trusted to treat them with tenderness and understanding.

Jesus, Our Truest Sympathizer

Jesus is the kind of high priest you turn to in times of need because you know you will receive mercy and find grace. He doesn't look at you oddly as though you were from another planet or say to you,

"I just don't get you. I can't understand why you would do something like that!" He sympathizes with your weaknesses.

Eugene Peterson's *The Message* captures the sense of verse 15 this way: "We don't have a priest who is out of touch with our reality. He's been through weakness and testing, experienced it all—all but the sin" (Hebrews 4:15 MSG).

Jesus walked in your shoes so he could share your experiences of temptation and suffering. He put his whole being into your sorrowful world so he can feel what you feel. He sympathizes with you because he lived through the same things you do.

He knows the frustration of days that don't go well at work. Or the gloominess that comes with physical illnesses in a body that starts to fail much too early. Or the uncertainty generated by natural disasters, economic instability, and nations struggling with each other. He especially knows the challenge of relationships that are often more a source of battles than of peace. And he understands firsthand how you are tempted to lash out, self-medicate, run away, manufacture your own diversions, or simply give up, hoping to be left alone. He was tempted in every way.

He feels your pain. He doesn't tell you to weep with others when you have had no experience of someone weeping with you. He doesn't expect you to create compassion out of thin air. Rather, he commands you to feel the pain of others based on your experience of him sympathizing with you.

Just Listen

One of the easiest ways to sympathize is to simply listen to the people around you. This doesn't always feel productive or even practical. Can just sitting with someone and hearing her story be of any benefit? Ask anyone who has suffered, and he'll tell you yes.

It is an amazing gift to have someone enter your world and care about the things you care about. By having someone listen, our loads are made lighter. This is difficult for Americans, who long to be productive, but it is a great gift to offer people who are hurting.

A dear saint who lost her husband of 40-plus years used to come talk with me. She didn't come to get any input or advice, but just to talk. She expressed her sadness over losing him, her joy over past memories that kept flooding her, her tears as she remembered the pain he went through, her laughter over things they'd done together, her difficulty with the silences that came from not having him around, and her loneliness.

She expressed her experiences because I was safe for her to unwind with. She didn't have to worry about how I was handling what she said. She didn't have to hold it all together for me. There was really very little I could do for her. Her family took great care of her, and the church loved her well. What I did was give her a place where she was allowed to be sad and I could be sad with her. Doing so helped lighten her load.

I remember the night I shared with my family that her husband, "Mr. John," had died. After hearing the story, my six-year-old son got up, came around the dinner table, and asked me, "Can I sit with you?" Let's think about that for a moment. Sitting with me did not change the situation—Mr. John was still dead and my son was still feeling his loss. I had not really done anything, nor frankly was there very much I could do, but my son was comforted because I joined him in his sadness and made it my own.

I shared that story of my six-year-old with a group in New Orleans. One of the people asked, "Is it really enough just to listen?" And I responded, "Yes, and sometimes it's the only thing you can offer. What do you think?" He agreed that it is extremely important. Only later did I learn that he is the Director of Disaster Relief for a mission agency. He knew firsthand that often listening is exactly what people need. Many times being with people and caring enough about their sadness to allow them to tell their story is all you can give. And it's often exactly what they need.

Here's the lie I think many of us believe: when someone is sad or grieving, I have to say something wise that will be really helpful. Who can live up to that standard? I certainly can't. If I thought I always needed to say something brilliant, I wouldn't bother getting involved in any conversations. By hard-won experience, I've learned that I don't have that much to say in difficult moments. But what I can offer is the willingness to have the conversation. You can too. Inviting the other person to tell his or her story is huge, and many times it's one of the few things you can offer.

Clearly, I'm not suggesting that people should wallow in their grief forever. *But,* following Jesus' lead, I see the weight of our God falling on the side of entering into each other's pain and sharing each other's sorrows.

This is a world full of sorrow. Paul tells us that we must go through many hardships to enter the kingdom of God (Acts 14:22). Everyone who owns Jesus as Savior is guaranteed to suffer. But God did not intend for his children to suffer alone. Instead, he planned that we would ease the burdens of our brothers and sisters, just as Jesus has eased ours.

Entering into Each Other's Pain

The early church understood the importance of entering into each other's pain and making it their own as they grew into a community. The word "sympathy" from Hebrews 4:15 appears later in the same book. In the passage below, it's translated as "had compassion on":

But recall the former days when, after you were enlightened, you endured a hard struggle with sufferings, sometimes being publicly exposed to reproach and affliction, and sometimes being partners with those so treated. For you *had compassion on* those in prison, and you joyfully accepted the plundering of your property, since you knew that you yourselves had a better possession and an abiding one. (Hebrews 10:32–34, emphasis added)

These early believers struggled with persecution. Sometimes they were the principal ones being persecuted. At other times they became partners with those who were mistreated and, in the process, had their possessions plundered. How did they become partners? They were led into it by their sympathy.

They had compassion—they were moved by what was happening to their brothers and sisters—and so they acted. That internal emotion led to action, which resulted in losing their belongings. If they had simply felt bad for those who were being persecuted but had done nothing about it, no one would have known their loyalties. A detached pity would have been safer. Sympathy, however, made them partners because it moved them to action.

They visited their fellow Christians in prison. Maybe they took food to them so they would survive. Maybe they visited to encourage them. For whatever reason, these people who had not been singled out for persecution put themselves in danger by visiting their brothers and sisters. Their compassion led them to do things so that outsiders recognized they were from the same group as those in prison. The persecutors concluded that if they were that closely allied with each other, then they should be equally mistreated.

These brothers and sisters had to know the dangers of their sympathetic compassion, and yet they acted anyway. They took on the other people's identity in order to bring them some relief—even if that meant adding to their own hurt. In other words, they felt the other person's pain and made it their own, just like Jesus had entered their pain and made it his own.

You can learn to do this even when you've been badly burned by someone close to you.

Ron knew all about being hurt. The woman he loved and had pursued for seven years turned out to be impossible to live with. Fierce, controlling, hypocritical, over-bearing, self-righteous, pushy—those are only a few words that describe the stories he told of life before he and Lauren separated. His protective response was to pull away from her as he grew more and more bitter over time. The bitterness, unfortunately, survived longer than his marriage.

One day he surprised me. As we talked he found himself on the edge of bitterness again, toying with insults and fantasizing what he wished he had said. But then, only ten minutes later, our conversation changed as he humbly said, "I wish there was someone to whom she could turn to get real help because, right now, there's no one in her life."

That was compassion for someone who had wounded him deeply. It was beautiful, but I wanted him to see how we'd gotten there so he could get there later on his own. I asked him to back up and help me understand what helped him change. If you follow his train of thought, you'll also learn how to sympathize with others, even when they hurt you.

He noted three things that are critical for developing compassion. First, he recognized that, as much as Lauren's issues had hurt him, they were hurting her even more, ruining not only her relationship with him but with all the other people in her life as well. He allowed himself to think about the effect she was having on her larger world and how that wasn't good for her.

Second, he thought about how he had been in exactly the same place as his former wife. He had his share of bad relational patterns that had contributed to making it hard to live with him. Despite that truth, Jesus had not abandoned him but had been kind to him. God cared for how Ron was hurt by Lauren—and he comforted his soul—but he also cared for how Ron had hurt Lauren by helping him see where he needed to change. Third, now that Ron could see he wasn't stuck blindly in those bad patterns, he wished Lauren wouldn't be either, prompting him to long for someone to come help her as he had been helped.

Very simply, Ron was learning to sympathize. He saw someone else's difficult situation, made himself consciously think of ways Jesus had cared for him in his own similar struggle, and let himself want something better for the other person. He was learning compassion from the master. You can learn too.

On Your Own

1. How have you experienced the reality that Jesus sympathizes with you in your weaknesses? Meditate on that truth and ask the Holy Spirit to make it more of a reality for you.

2. When was the last time someone sympathized with you? How did that experience help you see God a little more clearly for who he is?

3. Can you think of a time when you were moved with compassion for someone else? How did you express that? Was it clear to the other person that you and he were partners? What were the questions or actions that communicated your partnership to him?

4. Who needs you to weep with them now? Ask the Lord to bring people to mind or open your eyes to those who are hurting around you. In a fallen world, it shouldn't be too hard to find them.

CHAPTER 3

Struggling Love: Confessing Our Temptations to Each Other

The corollary to loving someone enough to understand her internal feelings and struggles is to share your own with her. In this chapter we'll look at how we need to be open and honest with each other about our internal struggles to build good, healthy friendships.

That's risky. If someone else knows the deep places of my heart, that person might hurt me, which makes arm-length relationships look far more attractive, even if they're useless.

Thankfully, Jesus paves the way by taking the biggest risk first. He allows us to know him at a level that goes well beyond casual as he voluntarily shares with us not only his thoughts, feelings, and attitudes, but the things that tempted him as well. As you come to know him at this more personal level, you are drawn more closely to him.

You will experience that same closeness with your friends as you take the lead to let people know what takes place beneath the surface of your life.

How (Open) Are You?

You can tell a lot about a person by the way he responds to the question "how are you?" There are some people who assume you are simply greeting them and they automatically toss back, "Fine. Good. I'm fine." Their response looks polite as it follows the present rules of social convention. Press them just a bit, however, and you can quickly run into a wall.

I've annoyed a number of teenagers over the years by following up with, "So, what makes you 'fine' or 'good' today?" Almost without exception, they scrunch their shoulders and say "I don't know." One friend from college had a stronger reaction. She verbally pushed me away by saying, "Sometimes I don't want to know why I'm fine. I just want to be!" In those situations, the socially acceptable response of "fine" or "good" is actually a rejection of relationship. It shuts down openness by saying "I don't want you to know more about me."

Other people respond to "how are you?" with some version of "here is what is happening to me." They do share their joys and sorrows, but they don't talk about how they are responding to those difficulties. They present a highly dramatic picture of life around them, but they don't speak of themselves as interacting with that picture. Rather, at best, they are passive participants to whom things happen. They remain unknown as the events of their lives take center stage. For them, responding to "how are you?" stays at the level of a complaint or entertainment, instead of developing into a deeper relationship.

A third way people respond to "how are you?" is to say "here is what I am doing." Such people are much more active in the way they talk about their lives. Not only do they recount the things going on around them, but they let you see how they are responding. This *is* real life sharing, and yet there is a deeper realm to which they don't go because they ignore what is taking place inside them. They essentially give you the equivalent of a videotape of their lives, but they don't give you their inside stories.

The above three responses are common, but they work against developing deep relationships because they prevent you from knowing the other person. Jesus gave much more information because he was longing for a much closer connection with his friends.

Jesus Shares His Heart

Think back to the time right after Jesus was baptized by John, when Satan came and tempted him (see Luke 4:1–12). From Luke's account you know an awful lot about that time of testing. You know his location: he was in the desert for forty days. You know what he was doing while he was there: fasting. You know he was hungry. You know that another person, Satan, was there and that a conversation took place. You even know the content of the dialogue between the two of them. You know so much that you could easily create a movie script and give stage directions.

But you also learn about elements of Jesus that are beneath the surface. You know that for Satan to offer the things he did, they had to be things that were tempting to Jesus. You know that Jesus would have liked to satisfy his physical cravings, that a shortcut to regaining the rule of the world could appeal to him, and that people recognizing his glory was something that could distract him from what his Father had called him to. As you read this passage you get a sense of what pushed and pulled him internally.

So here's the big question: how do you know all this?

There wasn't any other person present. John wasn't scribbling down notes from the sidelines. Peter wasn't there with a video camera. There wasn't even someone hanging out from the crowd who always seemed to be in the background. Jesus and Satan are all alone. So how did we get this information, especially the deeper look into Jesus' emotional and spiritual life?

Keep that question in mind as you consider the time just before his death, when he prayed in the garden of Gethsemane (Luke 22:39–46). You know the things he prayed. You learn that an angel appeared to strengthen him. You're told that he was in anguish and so he prayed more earnestly—he did not want what was coming. You know very intimate details of Jesus' life at one of his most difficult moments. Meanwhile his disciples were a stone's throw away, asleep. No one who would later record his or her memories of that night was there watching You know things about Jesus that you have no right or ability to know—things he did, things he said, even things he experienced in his attitudes and feelings, along with the specific nature of his temptations. How do you know all these things?

There are two possibilities. First, the Holy Spirit could have revealed them directly to Luke. That's possible. In fact, he has done that in numerous places in Scripture. A few examples of that are the creation of the world in Genesis 1 or the prophetic visions and dreams that people had. That could have happened here too.

I lean away from this view, however, based on how Luke describes his investigative method. Luke, who was a medical doctor by training, carefully researched Jesus' life based on eyewitness accounts (Luke 1:1–4). He gives you the sense that if what he was writing did not have a personal, reliable source, he wasn't going to include it in his narrative. That's the second possibility—that Luke heard all this from eyewitnesses.

The problem for Luke was that in these segments there were no eyewitnesses . . . except Jesus. Luke, however, being a contemporary of the apostle Paul, did not have the opportunity to interview Jesus. That leaves only Jesus' friends, but they were not physically present (or awake) at these times. If they knew, it was because Jesus had told them, and then they could relay those accounts to Luke.

What you have in these passages then is the product of relationship. It's the product of Jesus sharing his life with his friends at a deep heart level. He talked with them about the things he felt and experienced, the things that stressed him and tempted him.

That amazes me. Here are two accounts in which we need God to fill in the blanks—and he did. He did so either by Jesus sharing himself in normal ways by talking with his disciples or by the Holy Spirit extraordinarily revealing himself to Luke. (If he chose the more unusual supernatural approach, then my point is actually stronger about how much God longs to share himself.)

And what does he choose to share? He shares moments of extreme temptation, along with the specific content of those temptations. He parts the curtain of his soul to give you a glimpse of what takes place within himself. The way Jesus responds to "how are you?" is to say "here's what's going on inside me."

Is that the way you tend to respond to your friend whom you haven't seen in years? Or is it easier to talk about the kids, the house, the spouse, and mutual acquaintances you've both lost touch with? How do you respond to your kids, spouse, parents, and roommates when they want to know how your day went? Do they get to know you at a deeper level, or do you stay on the surface of your life?

Jesus doesn't give a brush-off answer to "how are you?" He could have said, "When Satan tempted me I quoted the Bible" or "I went off and prayed about it." Each of those would be true, and yet you would have a sense of having been cheated, like he was withholding himself from the conversation. Unengaged. Reserved. Unoffered. His friends would realize pretty quickly, "Oh, okay, I can't go there. I'm not allowed to know too much about you."

Instead, Jesus responds with, "Here's how I'm responding internally to what I'm experiencing. I want to honor my Father in heaven, *and* life on this planet is hard. I'm tempted to be pushed and pulled by what's happening. I feel jerked around, and here's how I'm handling it."

Jesus shared himself with his disciples. *And* he shares himself with you. Those conversations weren't simply for the guys standing around two thousand years ago. He made sure the accounts got recorded into Scripture. He wants you to know those things about him too.

Amazing! We are being invited into the Trinitarian community. Certainly there are places where Jesus cannot invite us. God is still high and holy, so superior to us that he is beyond our ability to understand—"transcendent" as the theologians would say. But recognizing his transcendence serves only to highlight that we should know *nothing* about him. To be invited to become familiar with the inner depths of our God is a gift that goes beyond words.

Do you see his heart here? He's not content to have a long-distance relationship where he hides himself behind a wall and gives you orders and rules from the other side. Rather, he longs to share himself with you so that you know him deeply, intimately, at a level that is almost frightening to consider. To know the inner workings of the one who created and sustains the universe is a scary proposition for me.

Scary and incredibly alluring. He actually wants me to know him? Not just know things *about* him—facts, figures, information—but to know him way down deep. That means if I'm satisfied only with managing a fair amount of data about him, I miss what he longs for. He longs for connection, to forge a bond with people. He doesn't do so out of his own neediness—you never get the sense that he will lose his bearings without human relationships—but out of wanting to share the best thing there is in the entire universe: himself.

Do You Long to Know His Heart?

Keep in mind with whom Jesus chooses to share his heart. The disciples are neither brilliant nor highly placed in their society. They're actually pretty clueless and calloused—rough around the edges at best. Often they don't seem even capable of being on the same page with what Jesus is saying. They're like you and me in many ways! And yet he shares himself with them. Isn't that amazing? Would you choose these guys—Peter? *Thomas?*—to unpack your deepest struggles with?

The one outstanding quality they do have is that they hang out with him. They want to be with him. At one point Jesus turns to the crowd in John 6 and says things that are so hard to hear that most of the crowd decides to leave. He then turns to his disciples and asks if they want to leave also, and Peter responds for them by saying, "Lord, to whom shall we go? You have the words of eternal life" (John 6:68).

What they lacked in brains and social refinement they more than made up for in heart. They wanted him. Outwardly, they were really nothing special, but inside they had a heart that longed for his heart. And so Jesus shared himself with them.

Did you ever date that special someone? If so, can you remember wanting to know everything you possibly could about him or her? Remember how that other person wanted to share? When my wife Sally and I were getting to know each other, we would stay up and out late at night (er, early morning) just talking—learning about each other. We were fascinated to hear another reveal depths of themselves that we would have no other way to know.

Your Creator and Redeemer wants to share *his* soul with you. He invites you to know him and relate to him by taking the first risk—he opens up and talks about what's going on inside of himself. That's an amazing, exciting offer. Knowing how badly he wants you to know him should stir you to long for him.

Sharing the Good, the Bad, and the Ugly

Notice that Jesus not only shares himself, but that much of his internal sharing revolves around the temptations he experiences. As amazing as it is to realize that he was tempted in every way just as we are (Hebrews 4:15), it's even more amazing that he openly talks about his temptations. The eternal Son of Man reveals the things that jerk him around.

Can you see him sitting around the fire at night or walking down the road talking with his friends about real life and the real struggles *he* faces? He's willing to go to a pretty deep level with these guys. "Here is what I struggle with. It's a real temptation for me to look for an easy way out so that I don't have to suffer." Jesus himself valued openness and honesty in his relationships.

How about you? Are you willing to know the Son of God at this level? Do you want him if he's going to talk like this? Be careful in answering because the flip side of the question is do you want to be known to the same depths that Jesus does? James 5:16 urges us to "confess your sins to one another." You are invited to a community where people voluntarily expose their inner lives to each other, even when it's not pretty.

> To love well, you need to take advantage of the (many) opportunities you're given to be open about your life.

If God doesn't think he can really be friends with you unless he voluntarily takes you into the deeper places of his being, then obviously this is a key element that needs to be in your human relationships as well. Without it, you are deciding to withhold yourself from others, which will guarantee that you rarely enjoy close, supportive friendships. To love well, you need to take advantage of the (many) opportunities you're given to be open about your life.

When my first book came out, I could hardly wait for it to be reviewed on Amazon.com. Many people had given me very positive comments on it as it had journeyed from infancy to production, and I was just waiting to see someone outside my circle post something about how good it was. (You see where this is going, don't you?)

Sadly, the first reviewer started by giving me three stars out of five. *Three out of five?* I thought. *It's better than that!* So I started reading and found, to my relief, that it wasn't an awful review. In fact it was pretty decent—until I got to one line: "At times the author did a superb job in intermingling Bible stories with real life stories, dealing with the same scriptural principal [sic]. More often than not, however, the flow of a chapter was unnatural as he attempted to weave the biblical principle into everyday life."

Ouch!

What do you mean "at times"? "Unnatural"?

Now, you need to know more about me. I don't do criticism well. Never have. I have had a long journey of learning to hear people better when I find out they are underwhelmed with something I've done. It's one thing, however, to hear criticism from an individual I'm counseling or a group of students in a classroom. But this criticism was published on the Internet. For *everyone* to see (well, actually only for those who stumble across one small, nondescript page out of millions, but still!). I was not having a good day.

A student called me a little later that morning. And she had the gall to ask "how are you doing?" How are you *doing?*

What were my options for an answer? *Good—fine. I'm good.* Just stuff down the way I'm feeling and the things I'm thinking and put on the charade of having everything all together. *I'm the Prof; you're the student. You aren't allowed to know me and what I struggle with.* Or I could've gone with the complaint response: *Oh, I'm really upset this morning. You should see what this guy wrote! What is he thinking? Why, I could get together 100 people who have been nothing but positive.* That way I could focus the conversation on the other person and completely ignore my feelings in the middle of it. Doing so would have been easy, and she probably would not have pressed me further.

Alternatively, I could have stayed at the external level of my own activity, *Oh, this guy wrote this thing and I'm not going to worry about it and just keep working. I've asked some people who have said positive things if they would weigh in and kind of balance him out. I guess we'll just wait and see how things work out. What can I do for you?* That way I would communicate "I'm okay. He's a loser, but I've got it under control. No needs here!"

Instead, I took a deep breath and went with the most open approach: "Here's what this guy said. And it gets to me. I tend to want everyone to be impressed with me all the time and he's not. On top of that, he's decided to share his less-than-impressed viewpoint with several billion people. So now I'm sitting here unable to work and wrestling with how I tried to write about the glory of God but am stuck worrying about the glory of Bill."

This gives a full picture: here's what's happening and here's what I'm doing because this is how I'm internally wrestling. By responding that way, I invited her to a relationship, to know me as a real person with real struggles, real difficulties, and real needs.

She responded to my invitation very simply by praying for me at the end of our conversation. "Jesus, I ask that Bill would not lose the joy he had when he was writing about you." That was exactly what I needed to hear. Her broader perspective helped realign me to what is important in life and helped me get back on track with what I needed to do that morning. By stepping into my life she reinforced to me one more time how desperately I need my Christian friends in order to live my life.

Are you looking for those opportunities to connect more deeply with others when they come up today? They will. People are relational creatures, which leads them to ask "how are you?" in the hope of really connecting with you. Are you answering in a way that will invite others in?

The Purpose of Openness: Experiencing More of Jesus

Responding well to someone's invitation is just as necessary to building close relationships as offering those invitations yourself. Perhaps, however, those invitations scare you because you're not sure what to do with them. Maybe you're afraid that if your neighbor were actually open and honest you'd have to respond, and you're not entirely sure how to do that.

Too many people fear that after someone opens up his life, their responsibility is to rush in and somehow give answers or solutions to what the other person faces. And so we shoot from the hip: "Okay, thanks for sharing that with me. Now here is what you need to think . . . here is what you need to believe . . . here is what you need to do . . ." Or we stand around uncomfortably, afraid of saying the wrong thing.

Such responses crush openness. If you're concerned that your primary responsibility is to give advice, then relax. Responding to someone's invitation to be known doesn't mean he is necessarily asking for your advice on how to handle his situation. You're off the hook.

Conversely, to build strong relationships you will need to do more than endlessly wallow in your experiences together: "Oh, I struggle with that too! I don't know what to do with it either but we can talk about our shared experiences of struggling." That response sounds better than quickly giving advice, but it lacks a redemptive spin. There's no sense of forward progress.

You probably have a few friends like this. Everyone ends the conversation having shared his story, but there's no real hope of life being different, and the conversation sort of drifts away to another topic or ends with everyone awkwardly staring at the floor. There has to be something more robust than that.

Let's go back to my example. Is my openness an invitation to my friend to tell me how to handle the review critic? Well, yes . . . and no. If I'm uninterested in receiving input from her when I share my life, then I'm not really being open. I'm not sharing my life in a way that invites the wisdom of Christ's friends to speak into my life. But if this lady feels that she has to give me advice since I've shared myself, she's missed the point of openness. Our mutual calling is to live out our faith together, not simply provide solutions to one another.

> *Our mutual calling is to live out our faith together, not simply provide solutions to one another.*

When someone opens her life to you, she's actually inviting you to a relationship—to growing together. Any answers and companionship in suffering you offer exist within the larger context of "we are on a journey together of learning to see and experience more of Christ in us as we live in his kingdom." Answers are important, but they're not the end goal. We do struggle together to make sense of life, but struggle is not the end goal. The end goal is to see a little bit more of Jesus than we did earlier.

That means when your daughter comes home and shares about her classmate who "accidentally" pushed her into a locker, you cannot simply respond by giving her techniques for dealing with bullies. You need to keep in mind the bigger picture of how this incident fits into your journey and your daughter's journey with Jesus.

A friend from church, Andrea, needed to talk to her boss one morning and she was really scared. He was not easy to talk to, and he hadn't come in that day in a good mood. Andrea tried a few times to start the conversation, but each time she lost her nerve before she got a word out. She sent me a text message that said, "You can cut the air in the office with a knife. Each time I go in there I freak."

I texted back, "How does Jesus respond when you go in there?" Please notice that there isn't anything about that question that requires highly skilled, therapeutic expertise. In fact, the only hard part about it is remembering to ask.

She replied, "He's disappointed when I bail."

Here's where her heart struggles. At a functional level, Andrea believes that Jesus is just like her boss, only maybe a tiny bit nicer. But, like her boss, all he does is demand impossible things of her (for example, confronting a difficult employer), but then stands back without helping her and is mostly unhappy with her.

Her text led us to reconsider how he promised never to leave her or abandon her, even in the presence of an overbearing boss. That conversation helped build her faith for what she needed to do. The time with her boss did not go well, but she experienced Christ in the moment and saw over the next several days many other ways that he was involved in her life for good and not for harm.

When she shared her heart with me, did I have answers? Not really. Did I understand how hard this was for her? A little. More than that, however, in sharing our lives together, we got to see where Jesus was and what he was doing.

That means when your friend opens up her life to you, first respond by simply appreciating her openness as an invitation to share your lives together. You say, "Thank you for trusting me with that. I appreciate you being vulnerable. I'm glad to get to know you a little more deeply." This affirms that her openness has not chased you away, but that you are moving toward her while she is moving toward you.

Next, ask questions that invite her to share more. I'm amazed at how often God asks questions when he could give answers. Loving others like I've been loved means I try to imitate him and learn to ask questions better. "So where are you with that?" "How are you responding?" "What are you doing with that?" Those questions tell your friend "I like the person you are, this person I am getting to know. I can handle what you're telling me about yourself. Please let me know more of you."

Thirdly, make sure at some point to ask "where is Jesus involved?" Ask this even if you're not sure what the answer is. Sometimes I have to add, "I don't know where he is, but I do know that we need to look for him. What do you think he is doing?" By asking the question, you're helping her think about where the next steps are on her journey with the Lord through life.

Leading in Sharing

Friendships in which people feel free to share their difficulties give them permission to drop their guard and ask for help as they grow into the fullness of Christ. But if you want to have those kinds of relationships, you have to take the lead in sharing your difficulties. Look for these opportunities and intentionally offer yourself to others.

Each month our church elders, deacons, deaconesses, and trustees come together for a joint meeting during which the pastors give a report from their various ministry spheres. Our desire is to share with the other elected ministry leaders what we believe God is doing among us. It's healthy accountability for the pastors, but it could easily become a dog-and-pony show if we were to select only those few highlights that cast us in the best light possible.

Even worse, by showing only positive aspects of our lives it would become a time that fostered less genuine relational connections. With that in mind, one night I shared that my wife and I were deeply concerned for one of our children. I didn't share a name or even gender information, but I did describe some of what we saw and concluded by saying, "Please pray for us to have extra wisdom and love for this person because this is well beyond our parenting abilities."

They did pray, and the next few days were easier at home, which was a huge relief to us. But there was even more relational benefit that came out of that time. Quite unexpectedly, one of the leaders approached me in the foyer on Sunday between services, and with people milling all around, he started sharing how he and his wife were also struggling with their children. He said, "I've always kind of known we weren't the only ones, but it's different when someone shares out loud the same difficulties you're facing. It was so helpful to hear that there are times when you don't know what to do either. I don't feel like such a failure, and I feel that there is hope for us too."

He and I connected more deeply that morning. We had been friends, but now we were more. We were on the same journey together and we both knew it. It happened simply because I was willing to be slightly open about what was happening beneath my smile.

This is something you can do too. If all you did was take one opportunity per day when someone wanted to know how you were to let her glimpse the real you, you would experience much deeper connections with those around you.

I'm glad that my willingness to be vulnerable about my life encourages other people to be more open and honest about their own. And yet, to be open with you, there are times when I get tired of sharing my problems. To my own ears, I start to sound like a whiner.

Over coffee one morning, I told one of our elders that I don't want to be the high-maintenance pastor. He responded, "Actually, I think that is your job description. You're the pastor of counseling. That means your job is to lead the rest of us in learning how to let other people see the mess that we all are. When you talk about your life, we're encouraged to come out into the light with our dirty little secrets that we're afraid to let anyone else know."

I thought about what he said and remembered how good it has been for me to have both pastors and friends take the lead in opening up their lives. Their willingness to be open has helped me learn to ask for the help I need. They learned from other human examples, but ultimately we all go back to Jesus, who in his awesome majesty was unafraid of earthly humility.

He talked to his creatures about his inner life. The creatures were infinitely below him on every conceivable scale, yet he didn't treat them that way. He invited them into a relationship far beyond their imagination, sharing himself in ways they never could know otherwise. And he has done the same with you. In doing so, he points the way for how we ought to share ourselves with each other.

On Your Own

1. Meditate on the fact that Jesus wasn't worried about people knowing how he could be tempted. What does his lack of worry say about the security of the love he had with his Father? What does it say about his desire to be known by others?

2. What keeps you from being willing to offer your temptations and inner struggles to others? Fear, worry, and pride keep many people from intimacy. Take some time to ask Jesus to renew your confidence in his love. Perhaps you also need to repent over caring too much about your image in other people's eyes.

3. Identify one or two people in your life with whom you think you could share your struggles and temptations on a deeper level so that you could continue to grow in your faith.

4. Who needs your help in learning how to talk about her struggles and difficulties? How will you learn to share yourself more with her—not in a phony, canned way (that's simply self-protection at a different level) but in a way that invites her to experience the goodness of deeper relationships?

CHAPTER 4

Forgiving Love: Covering a Multitude of Sins

Part of living in a fallen world is daily experiencing your closest friends taking you for granted, running roughshod over you, keeping things from you, using you, avoiding you, betraying you . . . in short, sinning against you. Frankly, it's not a question of whether your friends will fail you today, but when and how they will. (Unfortunately, you'll probably return the favor.)

That reality does not need to lead you to despair for your friendships, however. It doesn't for God in his relationship with you. Those moments when you sin against him become opportunities for you to taste once again his great love for you in the form of forgiveness. This chapter will look at how forgiveness is so important to God that he almost appears to go out of his way to invite opportunities to show it.

As surprising as it sounds, you can learn to look at being sinned against as an opportunity to build closer friendships. As those around you come to believe that you are characterized by forgiveness, you will see them feel more safe with you and confident that their failings don't spell the death of your friendship.

It's Hard to Keep Forgiving

Sadly, forgiving others is not something that comes as easily to us humans as it does to God.

Once upon a time, Ryan and Madison began a friendship in which they initially believed the best about each other. To show their good faith, they handed each other 100 friendship coins. And both were happy. In the early stages of their relationship, they continued giving each other more and more coins. Everything felt good between them as long as they both had big piles of coins.

Invariably, however, as time went on one of them would reach over and steal from the pile that he or she had given to the other person. Some thefts were small (say, three-coin thefts) while others were larger (twenty or thirty coins at a time). Regardless, once the coins were stolen, they could never be replaced. Even when one person tried to give them back, they just weren't the same as they had been. They looked and felt different—dirty, tarnished, bent—so different that the other person didn't value them as highly.

More and more, their relationship became characterized by those thefts. Instead of remembering the coins they'd been given, they would ruminate on the ones that had been stolen. As a result, both felt that their pile was smaller than it should be and they felt less like being friends.

Each one dealt differently with the loss. Ryan simply let his pile continue to dwindle. Most of the time, he didn't know what else to do. The way he saw it, there was very little he could do to keep Madison from taking the coins she had given him unless she really wanted to stop. So he kept hoping that she would stop stealing from him. But she didn't, and he didn't like being hurt, so he slowly started to withdraw and insulate himself from her. After only a few years he found himself wondering how small his pile could get before he decided that she just wasn't worth it.

Madison, however, took an opposite approach when Ryan stole coins from her. Her strategy was to work hard to try to prevent him from further reducing her pile. She drew his attention to the missing coins each and every time he did something wrong. She required him to endure marathon sessions long into the night that thoroughly hashed out every nuance of what had happened, hoping he would become so sick of the process that he'd think well beyond twice before he ever did anything like that to her again.

When that didn't seem to work, she took to repeatedly reminding him of his past failures—to punish him, slow down his next failures, and enjoy the self-pity of being wronged. And when he still didn't get it, she'd hand him an ultimatum: "You better stop or else I will . . . not talk to you . . . quit sleeping with you . . . walk out on you," and so on. And she carried out her threats, even spending nights at a hotel or taking extended "visits" to her parents.

As different as the two strategies looked, the end result was the same. Outwardly, Ryan and Madison may have still looked like friends, but it was only an appearance. The essence of their friendship had died under the double load of her mistrust and his pulling away.

The façade of their friendship was shattered when Jenna came along. She seemed really interested in giving Ryan new coins that made up for the ones Madison had taken, and so he decided to be friends with her instead.

Did God Set Himself Up to Be Sinned Against?

Can you relate to either Ryan or Madison? What's your favorite strategy for handling people's friendship sins against you? Without knowing you, I'd be willing to bet that God's strategy is very different from yours. In building relationships with people, he almost seems to invite us to sin against him:

The Lᴏʀᴅ God took the man and put him in the garden of Eden to work it and keep it. And the Lᴏʀᴅ God commanded the man, saying, "You may surely eat of every tree of the garden, but of the tree of the knowledge of good and evil you shall not eat, for in the day that you eat of it you shall surely die."

Now the serpent was more crafty than any other beast of the field that the Lᴏʀᴅ God had made.

He said to the woman, "Did God actually say, 'You shall not eat of any tree in the garden'?" And the woman said to the serpent, "We may eat of the fruit of the trees in the garden, but God said, 'You shall not eat of the fruit of the tree that is in the midst of the garden, neither shall you touch it, lest you die.' " But the serpent said to the woman, "You will not surely die. For God knows that when you eat of it your eyes will be opened, and you will be like God, knowing good and evil." So when the woman saw that the tree was good for food, and that it was a delight to the eyes, and that the tree was to be desired to make one wise, she took of its fruit and ate, and she also gave some to her husband who was with her, and he ate. Then the eyes of both were opened, and they knew that they were naked. And they sewed fig leaves together and made themselves loincloths. (Genesis 2:15–17; 3:1–7)

If you want to be characterized by forgiveness in your relationships, you'll need to see how important forgiveness is to God in his close relationships. Look at how much work and effort he expends to set himself up to be sinned against just so that, in forgiving, he can give people greater confidence in their relationship with him.

First, he gives his children a command without giving them a reason that explains his command. Why steer clear of this tree and not any other? What made it so special? They might be able to figure out that it had to do with trusting his thoughts more than their own, but there's an awful lot riding on their decision. What if they came to the wrong conclusion about why they shouldn't eat from it? With so much at stake, you would have given a little more information to your children, wouldn't you?

Then he lets Satan waltz into the garden of Eden although he already knows how dangerous and antagonistic Satan is. By this time, Satan had already corrupted one third of the angelic beings and convinced them to join him in rebelling against their Maker.[1] Surely it was no surprise to anyone that he would try to co-opt these weaker creatures as well.

If a dangerous pit bull known for attacking people wandered into your backyard where your children were playing, would you casually ignore it? Wouldn't you do everything in your power to drive it away, while at the same time rushing your children to safety? Why sit back and watch how things unfold?

But it's more than that. God actively goes out of his way to set up a dangerous situation. Why even create the tree in the first place, or command Adam and Eve not to eat of it? That's like putting candy on the coffee table and warning your three-year-old, "Don't touch." Or worse: inviting the pit bull in.

Then, when Satan is in the garden, God doesn't refute him. He could easily have shown up and calmly shredded Satan's arguments, addressed all his slanderous accusations, uncovered the half-truths, and exposed the serpent for the scheming, deceitful liar that he is. But he didn't do that. This God, who *invented* language as a pale reflection of how he communicates Father-to-Son-to-Holy-Spirit, wrapped himself in silence.

Lastly, he does nothing as his child toys with the idea of temptation in her mind. She gazes at the fruit . . . reaches up . . . pulls one off . . . takes a bite . . . offers it to her partner . . . who also considers his actions before joining her in sinning against his God. There were so many opportunities to step in and put an end to their rebellion—he could have nipped it in the bud, dashed the fruit from either of their hands, and brought them to their senses. But he didn't. He allowed them to proceed with their desires.

What would you do if your child were playing with a metal coat hanger and developed an urge to jam it into an electrical outlet? Or impetuously wanted to chase a ball that had bounced across a busy intersection? Would you sit calmly on the couch as you watched your toddler climb the bookcase? Or would you act? Of course you would move. You would not simply warn your child, but you would take clear, practical, physical measures to restrain your child's foolishness.

God didn't. Can you not hear the whole universe scream *why?*

God's Mercy Triumphs over Justice

Why, indeed. The answer to this question is crucial to the way you relate to others because it goes to the heart of how God relates to you. Some people have attempted to answer it, however, by missing the relationship he is building. Instead, they highlight the free will that God has given humans or argue that this was a means of showing how bad humans are when left to their own devices.

Those responses are always unsatisfying to me because they make an assumption I think is false. They assume that humans are the most essential part of the universe. We need to remember, instead, that the whole point of creation is to reflect the glory of God (see Psalm 19:1–4 and Romans 1:18–20). If you're going to ask why God did what he did, you have to ask the question from the Creator's viewpoint, rather than the creature's.

When you do that, you are drawn forward irresistibly to Genesis 3:15, where God curses the serpent by saying, "I will put enmity between you and the woman, and between your offspring and her offspring; he shall bruise your head, and you shall bruise his heel."

This earliest announcement of the gospel, that your God is coming to rescue you from the forces of evil, lets you see into his heart—and makes sense of what happened in the garden.

In allowing them to sin against him, they better understood him and the foundation from which he would relate to them—one of openhearted longing to have them back. Everything he did, he did for the sake of relationship.

His children rejected him. They replaced him with someone else. But he did not reject them. Instead, he promised freedom for humanity from its chosen alliance with Satan, along with the Serpent's destruction. Humanity would not be obliterated that day; rather, from within the human race God would raise up a deliverer. In very clear terms his children told him that they preferred to trust Satan's wisdom over his direction. And in even clearer terms he responded to their sin with grace and mercy. He did not treat them as their sins deserved.

Everyone already knew he was holy and righteous—that was what the fallen angels learned when he judged them for their rebellion. But now, something new was revealed that was previously unknown: as important as justice is to our God, mercy that builds closer bonds between persons is even dearer to his heart.

And yet, there's a horrible conundrum: the evil that allowed his gracious character to be revealed also separates me from him. Here's my misery as an image of God: I need righteousness if I am to be friends with this great God whose goodness in the face of evil makes me want him all the more. But having sinned, I've lost forever the righteousness I need. I'm now caught in an inescapable circle: I see his goodness more clearly, yet I'm further away from him.

And that's why Jesus came, as promised long ago. You can never regain on your own what you've lost, so your God proposes a trade: your evil for his purity. As 2 Corinthians 5:21 puts it: "For our sake he made him to be sin who knew no sin, so that in him we might become the righteousness of God." That's a pretty steep price God chose to pay so that you would know his heart. But he thinks it's worth it for you to know him; for you to be friends with him.

Allowing the Serpent into the garden created the situation for me to know his grace. That does not make God responsible for the sinful decisions I've made. I am not a puppet, nor is he the author of evil. It does make him responsible, however, for wanting the depths of his kindness to be known and experienced. When Adam and Eve rebelled, you learn that deep within the heart of God mercy triumphs over justice. And you would never know that unless they had sinned. The presence of real evil against a holy God set up the condition that allowed his real goodness to be seen.

Please don't think for a moment that he was less sovereign over creation in that moment. He did not suspend his plans to display his glory across the universe. The fall of humanity into sin fit well within his plan. He was not a negligent parent. He wasn't simply waiting to see what might unfold as though he were a disinterested bystander. The garden of Eden was an integral part of his plan to coax us to see him—the invisible God. It was his invitation to know him—an invitation to deep relationship.[2]

Do you view settings of sin as the ideal place for others to know more of your goodness? Or do you work hard to limit those experiences? Haley and Jordan were still in shock, trying to sort out the broken fragments of their marriage after the grenade of adultery had gone off. Bewildered, they confided, "In ten years of marriage we've never had one fight!" For them, a marriage in which they didn't experience disagreements or even times of tension was the evidence of a good marriage.

How is it possible for two sinners, despite being redeemed, to share a life together without being affected by one or the other's selfishness? It's not. But in making that their goal—sadly, in my experience, it's far from theirs alone—they lost far more than the opportunity to learn to work out their differences; they lost the opportunity to discover the other person's love remained even when he or she did something wrong. They didn't learn that God's way of strengthening relationships goes beyond merely doing the right thing.

God Reveals His Goodness in How He Treats Us When We Sin

God wants you to see how secure your friendship with him is by seeing how good he is when you're not.

Does this sound like I'm saying you should sin even more so that you can see his goodness even more? Paul anticipates that very objection in Romans 6:1: "What shall we say then? Are we to continue in sin that grace may abound?" He answers his own question, "By no means!" *But* he realizes that this objection is bound to be raised when you correctly unpack the exalted place of forgiveness in God's gracious, cosmic plan of redemption.

To my shame, no one has ever objected that way when I teach. And no one will, unless I come very close to saying that God invites people to sin against him so they can know him more intimately as they see him more clearly. That's what's happening in the garden. God does not solicit evil to come out of his people—he is not the creator of sin. *But* he sovereignly opens the door to being sinned against to show you his grace.

If the progenitors of the human race had obeyed perfectly, they would have experienced perfect fellowship with God—but it would have taken place at a shallow level. They would have been warranted in believing that God was good to them because they did everything right. They would have had no way to know that their relationship with God depended more on his goodness to them than it ever did on their obedience. They would never have known the security of a friendship based on grace, rather than one built on merit.

That wasn't enough for God. He longed for such a deep relationship with his children—one in which they knew core things about him—that he didn't create a world in which we would be perfect. Instead, he created a world that was perfect for displaying his character, a world that required him to take our imperfections upon himself to remove them, so that we could again be in perfect relationship with him.

Sin and rebellion are not good things—we may *not* sin so that grace may abound—but in redeeming sin, God's goodness is revealed in a way that we would never have known otherwise. One of the primary ways the invisible God reveals himself to you is in how he treats you when you sin against him. If that is so, you probably won't be surprised that he calls you to treat others in the same way, with the same graciousness, when they sin against you.

God's Ambassadors Now Cover Sins

Right before the verse in 2 Corinthians where we learn that Jesus trades his righteousness for our sin, we are urged to play a part in calling people to recognize God's grace. "We are ambassadors for Christ, God making his appeal through us. We implore you on behalf of Christ, be reconciled to God" (2 Corinthians 5:20).

You are an ambassador of this gracious God who is reconciling sinful humans to himself. That means your thoughts, attitudes, words, and actions should let people know clearly who your God is. When they see you, they should conclude that God would react exactly the same way to them as you are. That's why he's left you here. So how do people experience you when they sin against you?

I was driving to see Jaden. Normally I don't make house calls. In fact, he was the only person on my counseling schedule who didn't come to my office. I had called earlier in the day and gotten a computer-generated message informing me that "This customer has not yet set up his voicemail account." Not a promising start. But I drove the half hour to his workplace anyway.

Now, my life doesn't have a lot of spare half hours in it, so I was more than a little annoyed when I got there only to discover that he wasn't there. When I asked if anyone knew where Jaden was, I was told he was at another building—the one that I had passed a few miles back up the road. Gritting my teeth and trying not to be upset, I drove back to the other building, only to find him in the process of getting into his car with another employee! So, as any gracious ambassador would, I parked him in.

Trying to contain my irritation I asked, "Are we getting together today?"

To which he responded, "We can if you want to." If *I* want to? I didn't drive all the way out there for *me*. This was something *he* wanted. Again, I decided to resist any sarcasm by simply saying, "Yeah, let's do that."

To which he replied, "Okay, but I have to go back to the other building . . . and I have to stop at Pep Boys on the way."

"Oh, okay." I didn't trust myself to say anything more than that, but I sure did think some things on the way back. *We need to have a little talk. He needs to realize that my time is valuable and that I've got better things to do than joyride around in the middle of lunch-hour traffic. Maybe I should remind him that I'm one of his pastors. That I'm a busy man. That counseling sessions in the real world cost close to $120 a session. He needs to take this more seriously. He needs to take* me *more seriously.*

And then I paused as the reality of what I was planning to communicate to him sank in: "I'm way more important than you are!

Who do you think you are to inconvenience me? If you expect any-thing out of me, then you better get your act together and never pull a stunt like this again!" I realized with horror that those were the exact messages he had heard for years, and that I was about to go down the well-worn path. Maybe I'd have worded it a little more nicely, but the message would have been the same.

I was so glad for those fifteen extra minutes of cooling my heels in the parking lot while waiting for him. When you've been sinned against, giving yourself time to cool off and think before you react often keeps you from saying or doing things that will harm the relationship more. I took the opportunity to pray. *Lord, clearly what I've been rehearsing is the wrong solution. But I don't know what to do differently. How do I approach him with grace instead?*

Kindly, the Lord dropped in my mind the picture of a very gra-cious person I know, so I tried to copy him. Yes, Jaden and I needed to talk, but now I wanted him to see this gracious Jesus, not my inflated sense of self-importance. Don't be afraid to adopt someone else's example as your own. Initially it might feel unnatural, but that's because you're not practiced. A model gives you a place to start from, which you can tailor to fit your own personality.

When Jaden got out of his car, I greeted him with a big smile and said, "Hey, brother! I am so glad to see you today!" When he tried to explain that he'd been called in to the other building earlier, I responded by asking, "Okay, thanks, I appreciate you telling me that, but I'm troubled. What have I done that makes it hard for you to call me to let me know?"

That opening led us to a deeper discussion about how his past experiences still influenced his present relationships. He spoke about how he didn't reach out to tell people things that might upset them, about how he drove himself to overwork because "I'm afraid I'll dis-appoint my boss and he'll kill me." For most people, "disappoint" and "kill" are on opposite ends of the continuum, but not for Jaden. For him they are next-door neighbors.

My soft, genuine question led us to much more vulnerable places because he didn't feel the need to hide, guard, or defend himself from me. Instead, we grew closer. More than that, subsequent discussions showed that our conversation led to some new ways for him to live less fearfully of what people might say or do at work. And it all began with him sinning against me.

A few days later I experienced a similar incident with a staff member at work. Then a few days later, with one of my children. Each time, I was the one being sinned against, and each time (remarkably) I responded with kindness. Each time our friendships became closer than they were before.

As I reflected on those three experiences, I slowly started to realize that when others are good to me, there is no need for me to extend grace to them (in the sense of being kind to them when they don't deserve it). They need grace from me only when they're out of line. That means that the only context that anyone will ever have for experiencing grace from me is when she is in need of it—which is another way of saying when she sins against me. So if you want to be a gracious (grace-filled) person, expect to be sinned against. Otherwise, there's no need for love to cover a multitude of sins (1 Peter 4:8).

> ... if you want to be a gracious (grace-filled) person, expect to be sinned against. Otherwise, there's no need for love to cover a multitude of sins.

That's a hard verse. How well do you let love cover a multitude of sins? Many people are much better at letting a multitude of sins destroy love. One husband described it this way: "There's nothing big that she or I do against each other in our marriage. But the small things don't get resolved and so they pile up, waiting. There's a strain now between the two of us that builds. And so one little thing happens—a miscommunication on who's making dinner, confusion over whose turn is it to drive the kids, something left in the middle of the floor—nothing big, but it gets added to the stack and then we relate to each other based on the larger pile to which the little thing is connected."

Can you relate to him? I certainly can. It's hard to simply deal with the problem in front of you without trying to connect it to all the others that have gone before. All I need is one negative comment and I quickly remember things from the past that I thought were forgotten. Real, honest forgiveness is a challenge, but it's also the way other people see and experience Jesus from us and draw closer to us.

Anticipating the Sin of Others

Since a crucial element of being an ambassador for Christ involves covering other people's sins, you should anticipate being sinned against. That goes against the grain of how I've lived much of my life. Instead of welcoming opportunities to show God's kindness, I have worked hard to minimize the ways people are able to sin against me.

I have had countless conversations with my wife geared entirely toward this thought: how can I say this the best way possible so that we don't ever have this conversation again? I've tried the time-honored traditions of threatening my children so they won't dare cross me or, when that hasn't worked, the equally time-tested option of bribing them to leave me alone. With other people, I've tried bullying and intimidating when I can get away with it, or ignoring and running away when I can't. All of these approaches have one thing in common: they are strategies for making sure people won't sin against me.

Simultaneously, they are strategies for making sure people never see the grace of God from me either. Being his ambassador means that when you sin against me, you should see a reflection of his grace in me. Small, to be sure, but an accurate picture of him nonetheless. Conversely, when I work to insulate myself from others' failings, I take away the context that would let them see a likeness of Christ's merciful response to sin. Keeping safe from others carries the steep price of preventing them from seeing Jesus and trusting me.

That means that if you want to love people well, you have to learn to see people sinning against you as normal, daily opportunities instead of unusual, unwanted interruptions. Without becoming paranoid, you should expect people to sin against you instead of being surprised when they do.

This is vastly different from thinking it's a good thing to allow other people to walk all over you. Please keep the goal clear. You're not inviting anyone to sin against you; you are inviting the person who does to taste a gracious response to her sin. Calling you to move toward someone who wrongs you is very different from calling you to allow that person to abuse you. The goal is not to enjoy being hurt, but to enjoy giving someone a chance to see God's mercy *after* he or she has hurt you.

> The goal is not to enjoy being hurt, but to enjoy giving someone a chance to see *God's mercy* after he or she has hurt you.

In a fallen world you will not need to look for people to harm you, but when they do, make sure they have a chance to see Jesus. It's not a matter of "letting" others sin against you. They are going to. It's a matter of how you'll respond. Letting someone sin more so that grace may abound is just as stupid on a human-to-human level as it is on a human-to-divine level. There's a word for that kind of relationship. We call it codependent.

The kind of forgiveness you offer communicates the kind of relationship you hope to build. True ambassadors don't merely overlook the sins of another. They also call the other to be reconciled. When Jesus forgives you, he longs for you to move toward him. Similarly, when you forgive those around you, you are inviting them to move away from their sin and toward you.

Romans 2:4 reminds us that God's kindness leads us to repentance, while 2 Corinthians 5:20 reminds us that divine kindness invites divine reconciliation. Human kindness hints at divine kindness by providing an experience of human reconciliation. It suggests what life might be like if the other person were to respond. When I'm willing to cover your sins, I'm inviting you to care that you have hurt me and I'm inviting you to stop so that we can be reconciled.

Back to the Gospel

Unfortunately, if you're anything like me, there are days when you just don't want to forgive anymore. You feel assaulted by your children's slights and insults, taken for granted by the way your friend casually broke your date (again), or hurt that your husband only notices you in the bedroom. Sometimes—many times—forgiving others doesn't seem glorious or compelling.

Those are the times when I realize that, once again, something has become more important to me than living to promote the glory of God. I suspect I'm not alone. How many mornings have you awakened crying out for opportunities to show the glory of the gracious God to weak, fallen, and rebellious sinners? Instead, aren't you inclined to think much more about how to conserve your good feelings while minimizing the bad?

To reenergize yourself in your human relationships you need to relive the wonder of Jesus not treating you as your sins deserve. You and I will pass along to others only the amount of graciousness that we presently experience.

That may be a scary thought for you because it means admitting how much you would rather live for something other than to know Christ and make him known. You might be tempted to believe, "I don't think I could handle seeing how bad I really am. I don't want to forgive my coworker, although Jesus has forgiven me." Such an avoidance strategy is guaranteed to fail, however, because, in guarding yourself from seeing your sin, you also guard yourself from seeing Christ's kindness. The solution is to look not only at yourself, but even more at your God, who willingly took your sins on himself so that you could know him.

Once you find the forgiveness with him that you don't deserve, you won't be able to keep from giving it to that person who needs it from you. And when you do, you will be drawn together as you both more clearly see this God who thinks that knowing him is so special that he dares to forgive us.

On Your Own

1. How do you respond to this God who willingly lets you sin against him so that you can see the beauty of real grace? Do you find yourself wanting more of him—or less?

2. What has been your experience of the church? Has it been a community more focused on telling you how to live so that you don't need forgiveness or more dedicated to proclaiming the glory of knowing a forgiving God? How has that emphasis shaped the picture of God you now show others?

3. If you're going to show mercy to sinners, you will probably need to train yourself *beforehand* to respond well. How often

do you wake in the morning crying out to God to show you the ways that he has been gracious to you? Or asking him to help you respond to others with the grace he's given you?

4.   Think proactively about who is likely to need mercy from you. Who tends to push your buttons and when—family, friends, neighbors? How are they likely to go about it? Make yourself ask in the moment, "What would mercy look like here? How do I treat him differently than his sins deserve?"

CHAPTER 5

Longsuffering Love: Patiently Bearing with Each Other

No one changes overnight, despite the best intentions or the strongest desires to live differently. Even those of us who know Jesus still wrestle with a nature that fights against loving our neighbor like we love ourselves. That means all your relationships are with people who continue to sin.

A necessary aspect of love, therefore, is learning to live patiently with people as they continue on their own journeys of learning to live more righteously. That's what loving well is all about: giving people the time and space they need as they grow. This chapter looks at longsuffering love—the kind of love that hangs in there with people over the long haul as they sort out their issues.

Without longsuffering love, our holy God could never live in close communion with each of us unholy people who are not instantly sanctified when we're born into his family. It's necessary for his relationship with us. That makes it necessary for our relationships with each other.

This aspect of love takes seriously how hard it is to change and how much help people need from their friends in order to face their demons. It allows them to address their issues within a supportive environment that embraces them while urging them on.

Jake and Hannah would tell you how necessary longsuffering love from others was for them. One Friday evening, they remarried each other. It was not a traditional wedding service. There was no fancy dress. No wedding party. No walk down the aisle. No reception. Instead, there was worship—deep, meaningful, soul-satisfying praise to a God who has chosen to live with sinful, fallen, messed-up people while they grow. It was a celebration. Celebrating with them was the human community, the network of friends and family who had walked with them, wept with them, argued with them, and pleaded with them—all out of love for them.

Jake had carried into their first marriage a history of seeking comfort in sexual sin when his life was not going well. When he left Hannah and their two-year-old son for a homosexual lifestyle, he simply extended the patterns he had been building for years. Hannah was forced to move away out of financial necessity. The divorce went through uncontested. Her life became increasing unstable, as did her responses to it. His became increasingly dangerous. Chalk up another victory for darkness.

But God wasn't about to give up his people that easily. Two years were enough to convince Jake that he would find no more satisfaction in his new God-substitute than he had in all the others he had tried. So he returned to the church that had continued reaching out to him during his time away.

As he began dealing with the source of his problems, he longed for some form of reconciliation with his ex-wife. Amazingly Hannah was willing to move back into the area, with the understanding that she was not expected to remarry. That began years of living out their struggles in the context of people who loved them—numerous counselors, pastors, friends, and small groups. As they became more convinced that people were committed to them over the long haul, they both felt free to expose more and more of their issues and ask for help.

Slowly, their lives changed. Some counsel they accepted; some they rejected. Some was unhelpful, some was beyond their abilities, and some they simply didn't want. Sometimes they made important strides forward; at other times they did not. And yet those people close to them, their community, continued to patiently live with them as they worked through their personal issues.

Over time, Jake and Hannah became willing to live patiently with each other's issues. Initially, that kind of thinking was off the table because they each had too much to wade through personally. But later, the possibility of a relationship became an on-the-table topic. Then it quickly shifted to off again. Then on—then off. Then after cycling through that maddening sequence several more times, slowly, quietly, they rebuilt their relationship, until the Friday evening when their community witnessed their re-union.

Sadly that evening of worship wasn't the last word. Nearly two years later their marriage fell apart again. Life is like that, isn't it? Very few of us—none of us—live fairy-tale endings. But that harsh reality was another opportunity for their community to live patiently with them. On this planet you never outgrow that opportunity. Living "happily ever after" is not the goal. Living well with broken people is.

> Living "happily ever after" is not the goal. Living well with broken people is.

This is a story of two broken people who are learning to patiently live with each other's brokenness. More than that, however, their relationship is set within a larger circle of ongoing friendships. It's also a story of a community, a group of people who gladly bear with each other's failings because they know how Jesus lives among them with their brokenness.

God Builds Patience into the Way He Relates to Us

Given the breadth and depth of human sin, Jesus could easily have spent his entire life merely pointing out people's failings: "Peter, that wasn't a very kind thing to say just now." "Thomas, don't you know you're commanded to rejoice?" "You're slandering again, James." "Oh, and *you*, you got this wrong and that wrong." "*You* did wrong. *You* are wrong." "When are you people ever going to do anything right?" Surely there was enough material around for him to be a machine-gun critic if that had been his interest.

But that kind of person drives people away. Never once do you get the impression that people could barely stand to be around Jesus. Instead they swarmed to him—*not* because he always told them what they wanted to hear. He wasn't soft on sin. He did point it out, but he didn't do so constantly, certainly not to the extent that it was present all around him. He was neither prickly nor critical.

Instead, he lived among sinful, imperfect, immature human beings, offering his friendship to them while they continued to wrestle with their radical imperfections. He neither crushed them nor drove them away. Watching him brings clarity to what his Father did many centuries earlier in the wilderness.

When God liberated the Israelites from Egypt he made a covenant with them. He reminded them in Exodus 20 of his relationship to them, that he is their God and he alone will deliver them from slavery and death in Egypt. After revealing his heart for them as their defender and deliverer, he gave them commands so that they, in turn, would know how to live with him.

Moses relayed the Lord's words to the people and wrote them down. He then led them in a ceremony involving sacrifices and peace offerings where they joined themselves to God by accepting his covenant with them. Moses sprinkled blood on the people as well as on the altar that symbolized God's presence. They were now in a special, consecrated relationship with their God.

The only thing missing from the ceremony was a meal. Meals were often the way that a covenant was ratified and solemnized.[1] By eating together, the two parties emphasized *and* experienced the peace that the covenant created between them. So, having been given the covenant, the elders went off to eat . . . with God.

> Then Moses and Aaron, Nadab, and Abihu, and seventy of the elders of Israel went up, and they saw the God of Israel. There was under his feet as it were a pavement of sapphire stone, like the very heaven for clearness. And he did not lay his hand on the chief men of the people of Israel; they beheld God, and ate and drank. (Exodus 24:9–11)

As his invited guests the elders ate a meal that consummated the covenant he had just made with them, but they got so much more. They experienced the most intense pleasure that there is in or outside of the universe—they actually saw God—all at his initiative. The leaders didn't waltz presumptively into his dining room as though it were their idea to go on a sightseeing tour. They responded to God's earlier invitation to come into his presence (Exodus 24:1).

That taste of him foreshadowed his plans to have his presence dwell in the tabernacle, set in the very center of their community. By giving the elders as much of himself as they could stand (for no one can see God and live . . . yet!), he gave them a taste of what it would be like to have him live among them.

Don't miss, however, that he invites them into his presence knowing that everything in their lives and hearts is not okay. God did not raise his hand against the elders, but he would have been justified if he had. Remember, the blood of bulls and goats they had just been sprinkled with made them outwardly clean but could never take away their sins (Hebrews 9:13; 10:4).

Nor did it remove their ability to sin. In just a few days they would reject this God, whom they had just three times promised to obey (Exodus 19:8; 24:3,7). And while the depths of their depravity and betrayal may have surprised them, God wasn't shocked. Instead, he had already chosen to work with them through Moses, the very man who would be able to successfully intercede for them.

He knew his people were going to fail and had already made plans for their failings. Not only would they live imperfectly with a holy God, but they would live imperfectly with each other. They would still grumble about their wives, break promises to their kids, and start fights with their neighbors. That's why he created ways to deal with the sins they would commit against each other. He accepted sacrifices from them as an expression of their faith that he would pardon their sins. The very act of creating a sacrificial system to take away sins was a sign that he knew they would continue sinning throughout their generations.

Those sacrifices, detailed in the book of Leviticus, pointed toward what Jesus would one day do for them. This book, which was given at roughly the same time as he covenanted with his people, answers this very important question: how do we handle the ways we sin against God and each other so that we can still be part of his family? Even while God invites the elders to eat in peace, he's already planning to deal patiently with their failings—to share himself with them while they slowly mature in their faith. They will have to learn to deal with each other in the same way, which is exactly how we have to live out our relationships. Some things never change.

Measuring Progress

Maybe we should learn to measure progress in years instead of hours. Decades instead of days? It seems that's the clock God set to use with the elders and continues to use with me. He called his people to learn how to live well with each other even when they sinned against each other. He set the pace for those longsuffering relationships by inviting imperfect people to enter his presence and eat with him without being destroyed.

That's a glorious vision . . . and a hard reality. Living kindly and graciously with the people around you while they grow more mature in their faith is messy and time-consuming. You find things you didn't expect, things that make you shake your head and wonder if it's all worth it. It regularly takes more effort than you thought it would. It's not glamorous work, and it doesn't draw big headlines or attention. On top of that, many times it doesn't look like you're accomplishing much.

For those reasons, we're often too busy in the American church to want to put in the time and effort. It is so much easier to take the well-traveled paths of ignoring the problem or shunning such people until they're either shamed into leaving or pretending they've got their life under control again.

Too often, we treat sin like it is an unexpected surprise—an aberration that no one could have foreseen—when nothing could be further from the truth. God has gone out of his way to let us know that despite how hateful sin is, it sadly remains one of the realities of life in this present age. Until Jesus returns, you and I will wrestle with our own sinful inclinations, *but* he doesn't expect us to do it on our own. When people fail, their failure doesn't disconnect them from each other. Instead, their individual problem becomes a corporate opportunity—an opportunity to love and be loved in a way that leads to restoration with each other.

> When people fail, their failure doesn't disconnect them from each other. Instead, their individual problem becomes a corporate opportunity—an opportunity to love and be loved in a way that leads to restoration with each other.

An elder was sharing with me one day that he and his wife thought the secret to the success of their 27-year-long marriage was that they had learned how to be patient with each other. He went on to say that he thought that was similar to our calling in all our relationships in the church. The goal is not to find the latest, greatest way to turn people into model Christians but to love well the imperfect Christians in front of us.

He was advocating that the church community learn how to run the marathon of Romans 15:1: "We who are strong have an obligation to bear with the failings of the weak, and not to please ourselves." This is different from "putting up with" whatever people are doing, which smacks more of tolerance or dysfunction than Christ. "I need you to like me, so I'll accept whatever you do." The calling is more like "I love you; therefore, I mold myself around your weaknesses so that you grow strong enough for the things God has called and gifted you to do."

Slowly I have come to realize that my calling in every one of my relationships is to live with sinful people the rest of my life. Like me, each person in my life is weak or sinful in some way. But that doesn't mean I am supposed to manipulate or nag them. Instead, I am to bear patiently with the things that are difficult for me to accept or that annoy me. *Not* to condone sin, but to realize frankly that people *do* sin and will need help. I am called to create healing relationships to care for those who are damaged, rather than throwing away the damaged or seeing them as an embarrassment.

Communion Reminds You of God's Patience

God has the same calling for you in your relationships, but who is equal to it? If you and I are to attempt loving as he does, we will need a much better resource than the brief mountain meal that God gave Israel's leaders. Thankfully, we have one. Today, God's people also eat a meal in his presence, one that celebrates the covenant he has made with us through the blood of Jesus. We call it Communion. The meal in Exodus and all the other meals throughout Scripture are mere shadows of this meal of peace.

It's a meal that remembers what Jesus did so I can be friends with God. But as I remember what he did, I also have to remember why he did it. Jesus died for me *because* I'm a failure. When I take the Communion elements, I announce to myself, to those around me, and to my Lord that I am a mess. I also announce that I didn't get over being a mess simply because Jesus rescued me. I won't ever get over my need for his death and resurrection. I won't get past it. I won't outgrow it. That's why we repeat Communion so frequently.

Sharing in Communion is one of the most authentic, honest activities you can participate in. When you remember Christ's death, you remember and re-proclaim your own weaknesses, failures, and moral inadequacies. You proclaim that you just cannot do it on your own. That you don't need a jump start for a dead battery—you need an entirely new engine block. The days I'm surprised at how big a mess I am are the days I've forgotten the faith I say I believe.

But while I proclaim my need, I also announce that in a very important way, God is okay with me being a mess. If he weren't, he would never have told you to keep Communion until he returns. That shows you the nature of his heart. He's not scowling, barely putting up with you. He's inviting you over and over again, "Come over here! Come and get what you need! Come and eat in my presence. Be fed on far more than a mouthful of cracker and juice."

In other words, he never expected that you would be perfect by now, yet he still longs to live with you. He isn't surprised that you need Communion again, and he is under no delusion that a time is coming in this life when you won't. He continues to offer to live with you and share himself with you, despite your ongoing imperfections.

He still cares about your holiness. He's okay with you being a mess, but that's not the same as handing you a license to indulge every lust or immoral inclination you can dream up. Those things are responsible for murdering Christ, for attempting to remove his presence from this planet. As such, they are the antithesis of relationship with him. They show that you want to be rid of him. Any hint of them in your life indicates there was a moment when you desired something other than his presence.

But if you are friends with Jesus, the presence of ungodliness in your life brings you remorse because you really do want a friendship with him more than with anything else. If that's you, Communion helps you realize that he doesn't hold those disloyal moments against you, even though by rights he should. He continues inviting you to a relationship with him, despite knowing dividedness will remain in your heart while you are on this earth.

Those simultaneous proclamations of my need and his invitation realign me personally to live my daily life by faith, but they take place among my relationships with others. Paul reminds us in 1 Corinthians 10:16–17 that, while we individually participate in Christ as we receive Communion, we do so as part of one body. Communion is not a solo undertaking. Being transformed into God's likeness—while on our way to live with him forever—happens as we journey together in hopeful, hope-filled relationships.

People around You Need Your Patience

Having experienced his patience with our failings, we must pass along that experience to those around us:

> Put on then, as God's chosen ones, holy and beloved, compassionate hearts, kindness, humility, meekness, and patience, *bearing with one another* and, if one has a complaint against another, forgiving each other; as the Lord has forgiven you, so you also must forgive. (Colossians 3:12–13, emphasis added)

I therefore, a prisoner for the Lord, urge you to walk in a manner worthy of the calling to which you have been called, with all humility and gentleness, with patience, *bearing with one another in love*, eager to maintain the unity of the Spirit in the bond of peace. (Ephesians 4:1–3, emphasis added)

And we urge you, brothers, admonish the idle, encourage the fainthearted, help the weak, *be patient with them all*. (1 Thessalonians 5:14, emphasis added)

There is a very important assumption underlying each of these commands: people, including Christians, will make your life difficult—regularly and often. If that weren't true, there would be no need for repeated instruction to bear patiently with other people. The reality is that even blood-bought, Holy Spirit-filled believers sin. They sin often and they often sin against you. Therefore, you need to bear as patiently with them as God does with you.

That's hard, but necessary, if you're going to build relationships with others like he builds with you. Bearing patiently with your friends brings them hope—people often know they're not right, but they don't always have confidence that other people can help them when they're not.

I had barely been home ten minutes after a long day when one of my children was literally yelling at me. I don't understand that approach to life, and my first impulse is to distance myself from it, either emotionally or physically. But this particular time, despite being tempted to respond with my own version of upset, I had a deeper longing to handle the situation with gentleness and grace.

So I listened and asked questions. In doing so, I quickly learned I wasn't the cause of the frustration. Instead, a school project was due and there was no way to complete it at home because we didn't have the Internet. So my child exploded, pressured between a deadline and a lack of resources. But by treating my child gently—not counting her sins against her—we arrived at a solution that calmed her heart and addressed her frustration.

Those are beautiful moments when you can step outside of the immediate moment and bear gently with someone else. Where instead of taking personally the (very) personal attack, you respond with patience and gentleness. And therein is great hope. Patience is not simply one of God's virtues that he has showered *on* you; it's one of the things that his Spirit causes to grow *in* you.

The expression "I have run out of patience with you!" is misleading. It invites you to think of patience like a mineral deposit: once you mine it out of the ground, it's all gone. Instead, patience is more like an organic resource. It grows in proportion to your need because it's produced in you by the most fruitful farmer there is.

Jesus died to ensure that you'll be with him forever, which gives you hope even when you've "run out of patience." He has committed himself to seeing that you keep maturing—that you grow in bearing patiently with others. If you have any longing, even if small, to be more patient with those around you, then rejoice. That desire is an indication that he's already at work in you.

> *The expression "I have run out of patience with you!" is misleading. It invites you to think of patience like a mineral deposit: once you mine it out of the ground, it's all gone. Instead, patience is more like an organic resource. It grows in proportion to your need because it's produced in you by the most fruitful farmer there is.*

Practical Aspects of Bearing Well with Others

There are several things you can do in response to the desire God grows in you to be more patient with other people. First, carefully identify where you're not patient and why you're not.

It was a bad day when I came in from being irritated with the kids. They were playing in the front yard . . . again. Trampling the grass that wasn't growing . . . again. After I had talked with them that morning about staying off it . . . again.

So I was already primed for a blowup when I walked into the living room and discovered crumbs of chocolate cake on the three C's that are to be regarded as sacred—coffee table, carpet, and couch. And I lost it. I let everyone in the room under five feet tall know how unhappy I was. But throwing a tantrum didn't take away my impatience. As I tried to clean up the mess, I felt my blood continuing to boil. Those warning signs meant Daddy needed a time-out, so I went and sat on the back patio.

Sally came to talk, which did help me calm down. Somewhere between talking with her, talking with Jesus, and mentally replaying what I'd done, I knew that I was wrong. I could hear the harshness in my voice, see the sternness in my face and eyes, and realize how severe I'd been. What they'd done wasn't right, but I could now see where I was more wrong. If you're going to learn to bear patiently with others, you need to be willing to hear when you haven't done so.

I'm hopeful after having blown it because I know that Jesus bears patiently with me even in *those* moments. I know that I haven't lost his friendship—although by rights I should have—so I can repent to him and quietly go back inside to ask my children's forgiveness as well.

A second part of bearing patiently with others involves working to reconnect with the people around you. Impatience blossoms when some*thing* becomes more important than some*one*. In those moments, you need to offer to take the focus off the thing that caused the problem and remind both of you that your relationship is more important.

After I asked one of my sons to forgive me, I asked if he wanted to take a walk. I swore to myself that I would not bring up any of his failings during that time—those from the immediate present or the past. This was simply a time to reconnect with him.

As we walked, I knew I couldn't take away what I did or said. Worse, I could not remove the memory of that experience from his mind. But I could offer—not beg—to make new memories. Offers that say "I want to live at peace with you. I want another chance to be friends." Offers that give hope that the relationship is not over. You can't make the other person take you up on it, but you can offer to reestablish the relationship.

Lastly, you need to continually reorient yourself to bearing patiently with others. I'm not very good at that lifestyle. Frustration, annoyance, and dissatisfaction with people come much easier for me. Too often my face and my voice let others know that I think they've just caused me one more irritation I didn't need. An assistant once noted that I had the loudest sighs she'd ever heard—apparently you could hear them throughout the building. *Not* bearing patiently with other people's shortcomings comes easily to me.

That means I need to be reminded regularly of the goodness of God's ways because they don't come naturally to me. I need pictures of what this might look like. I need pictures that help me see why I would want to lay my life down for the sake of others. Pictures of what it means to be gentle with people when they're not at their best. Pictures that make me long for a life I'm barely beginning to understand.

One night I dreamed I was interacting with a person I had never met. She was mean-spirited, nasty, and difficult to get along with. Despite all that, I responded kindly and gently to her (which is the evidence that it was a dream). She, in turn, lost her hostility as she became more secure and trusting in the relationship. Instead of being prickly and defensive, she became my friend. When I woke up, I remember thinking, *Wow! That was really attractive! If that's what goodness looks like, I want to be that kind of person. I want to learn to be more kind to people when they aren't kind.*

Pictures like that don't mock me and my failures. Rather, they give me reasons for why I would want to continue learning to be patient. They are hopeful pictures for me because they show me where I am most certainly going. To be sure, my progress is slow, but it is certain and steady because my God is patiently bearing with me as I learn to relate to others like he does to me.

On Your Own

1. Think back to how long you've wrestled with some areas in your life—there are vestiges of sin I can trace back for decades! What does it tell you about Jesus when you realize he still invites you to enter into communion with him? How has his unrelenting involvement changed you?

2. Bearing patiently with brothers and sisters goes to the heart of what church is all about. Have you had the experience of other people coming alongside you and loving you as you worked through an area in your life? What was that like for you? Did they help you see Jesus more clearly or did they cloud your understanding of him?

3. How would you rate yourself on the patience meter (1 = none at all; 10 = will go countless extra miles)? Could you share a recent example of how Christ has helped you bear with someone else's failings?

4. Who around you needs to see Jesus' brand of longsuffering? What might be some first steps to show them the goodness of long-term, patient friendships?

PART II

LOVE THAT REACHES OUT
TO BUILD OTHERS UP

God calls you to master the aspects of loving well that allow you to care for your friends, despite the fact that they are affected by sin and suffering. But love is more than simply reactionary. Jesus worked hard to build up his friends so that they could mature into the people God meant them to be. He encouraged, he instructed, he served. And they did the same. They became proactive. Not in a heavy-handed, cultic manner, but for each other's best interests.

From the first, ever since he goaded Cain into murder, Satan has urged families to destroy each other. At long last, God has reversed that dynamic. Cain asked rhetorically, "Am I my brother's keeper?" God's long-term, redemptive response involves re-creating relationships in which we do look out for our friends to benefit them.

In Part II we will look at the various facets of loving well that invite you to extend yourself to nurture someone else. Sometimes these aspects will immediately affect your relationships. But more often, they will work over time to create a context that lets the other person know you want what is best for her. They communicate "I am in this relationship with you for your good. I am not against you. I am for you."

Chapters in Part II

CHAPTER 6

Partnering Love: Working Together to Care for Each Other

An important aspect of loving people well involves moving toward others for the reasons God intended. When you build your relationships with his goals in mind, your expectations of others will be in line with what healthy relationships can offer. When you don't, you will tend to want more from your friendships than they can provide, leading you to respond in destructive ways. This chapter looks at partnering love, the kind of love that forms the basis of solid relationships by understanding why we're friends.

Jesus calls you "friend" not because he shares the same likes and dislikes as you, but because of a common love for his Father. By being friends with you he forges a common foundation for your other relationships, while simultaneously showing you the purpose of those friendships. The result is that you don't overload your present relationships by expecting more of them than they can supply and you extend yourself to people you ordinarily wouldn't.

The Dangers of Overvaluing Compatibility

Partnering love goes against the grain of what normally draws people together. Many people I've talked to wrongly believe their friendships are supposed to grow out of natural, easy connections. That belief makes sense to many people. You tend to look for close friends from among those who fit into your own tastes or lifestyle. You find easy connections with people who share your favorite hobbies, interests, leisure activities, philosophies, politics, values, foods, occupations, sports teams, and vacation spots. Unfortunately, despite being less difficult to begin, relationships built primarily on those things can easily pull apart when the resulting closeness is less than you anticipated.

Nick believes his wife is supposed to be his soul mate and is unhappy because they just don't seem to "click." Their relationship seems more arduous than effortless, which discourages him. Nick is not alone. Many men and women are dissatisfied in their marriages because they don't have the easy, deep affinity with their partner they were hoping for.

Some spouses respond by withdrawing into themselves and their hobbies. Others become increasingly demanding as they insist their partner live up to their expectations. "Why can't you be more _____?" they ask. Still others wonder if there are greener pastures to be had with someone else. Different responses; same result. Because they expected the relationship to be something it was never meant to be, they end up pulling away from the person they had worked so hard to unite themselves to.

It's not only in marriage that people try to build their relationships on weak foundations. Megan really struggled with loving the people around her. She recalled fondly how close she and Anaya had been. They'd shared similar values, interests, and life experiences. Then Anaya had moved away—far away.

Though she looked, Megan could not find a replacement. No one living nearby closely identified with the things she felt and experienced. Consequently, she ignored the people who wanted to be her friend because she didn't want *those* friendships. She wanted different relationships, with important, interesting people pursuing her who could share deeply satisfying, fulfilling interactions.

While I understand Megan's and my other friends' longings—having had them far too often myself—I am very thankful that God doesn't use their measuring stick to assess his friendship with me or with them. Instead, he lives right now in friendship with a wide variety of people and personalities whose differences far outweigh the similarities with him. He does more than simply tolerate us; he works to develop deep, ongoing connections with each of us. And he befriends us even when we're not friendly toward his other friends.

By looking at the nature of Christ's friendships with us, we will understand better how to build relationships with others, even when people don't perfectly suit our own likes and dislikes.

Jesus Calls Many Dissimilar People "Friends"

I wonder how surprised the disciples were when Jesus called them friends. They clearly thought of Jesus as their Teacher, Lord, or Master. And Jesus thought that was appropriate. He illustrated his lessons with examples of masters and lords with their students and servants that clearly pointed to his relationship with them (as in Matthew 10:24–25; 24:42–44; and John 15:20). He also affirmed his identity directly: "You call me Teacher and Lord, and you are right, for so I am" (John 13:13). How very odd then for him to say just a few minutes later, right before his death: "No longer do I call you servants, for the servant does not know what his master is doing; but I have called you friends, for all that I have heard from my Father I have made known to you" (John 15:15). Friends. Those who know everything he knows. Shared knowledge. Shared goals. Shared lives. The disciples are not minions sent to run errands they don't understand. Now they are elevated to the same status as Abraham, the friend of God (2 Chronicles 20:7; James 2:23). Jesus spoke to them face to face. That was what set Moses apart from all others and made it clear that he too was God's friend (Exodus 33:11).

They suddenly found themselves in the same company with Abraham and Moses. I bet that created a hush around the table— the bashful silence that descends far too infrequently upon the children of men, when they can't believe their good fortune but are secretly delighted with it all at once. Friend . . . roll it around in your mouth. Savor it. Friend . . . of the most high God.

If they had any doubt that they were really his friends or thought that he might be using hyperbole, he was about to put that fear to rest. Soon he would make the ultimate sacrifice for them: his life for theirs. He had just told them that no one could have more love than that (John 15:13). Truly, he was their friend.

And it was their friendship with him that drew them to each other . . . because nothing else did. These men could not have been more different from one another. Consider their occupations, ages, and political affinities. They were all very different and yet all united around this one person who decided to befriend them. If their ability to work together had been based upon a shared compatibility between them, the church would never have gotten off the ground. Instead, their close horizontal relationships grew out of their mutual vertical one.

God did not rely on some form of compatibility among these first twelve friends of his to ensure the success of their relationships with each other. When you think about how different they were, it's kind of amazing that they could manage to do something as simple as sit and eat peacefully together.

Even after they banded together to spread his kingdom, he never let their relational connections get any easier. He quickly added three thousand more friends who didn't speak the same language—sharing a meal just got harder once again (Acts 2:41). Then, once they got themselves sorted out, he added Gentiles into the mix, and now there was no way they could even think about having dinner (Acts 11:2–3).

God doesn't prize compatibility for our closest and dearest relationships as highly as we do. Your involvement in the lives of your closest relationships was never meant to be built on a mutual like or dislike. It's not supposed to be built on your favorite hobbies, restaurants, department stores, or stage of life. Instead, the nature of your vertical alliance with Jesus is the single most important determining factor for all of your horizontal friendships.

This is not the same as saying "Don't have any friendships outside the church" (1 Corinthians 5:9–10). But you do need to recognize that your most important human relational clusters are based on the type of relationship you have with your Maker. Your shared horizontal relationships are dependent on a shared vertical one because your vertical relationship defines who you are, what you value, and where you're going. Therefore, you can develop close, satisfying relationships with people who on the outside, seem to have little in common with you—because you have the same core.

Will you be drawn to similar people? Of course. But I do think a corrective in what we value in friendships is long overdue. God is good at befriending people who are very different, then calling them to befriend each other. He desires that his friends develop diverse, complementary relationships with each other that go deeper than sharing a similar socio-economic status.

Your relationships with the people around you can transcend

the surface similarities and differences by prizing instead a shared friendship with Jesus. Rely on that shared passion for him more than your shared interests to bond you with people. It *is* natural to enjoy spending time with people who look, act, and sound like you do. But remember that God often calls you beyond what comes easily.

> It is natural to enjoy spending time with people who look, act, and sound like you do. But remember that God often calls you beyond what comes easily.

Take a moment to consider if you've fallen into the trap of believing that compatibility is the most important value determining how you interact with others.

Learning to Value People I Don't Like

"Okay," I can hear you say, "but I'm at the point where I don't even like the people around me, much less think of them as friends. What do I do about that?"

Let's be honest. There are many times when you're not sure how to even put up with the people around you, much less enjoy getting along with them. Furthermore, some of the people whom you regularly come into contact with can seem quirky, freaky, uptight, or weird—pick your favorite adjective for "someone I wouldn't normally choose to hang out with on a Friday night." Sometimes the people around you are hard to want to befriend.

In those moments you need to practice being confident that God knows better than you do who you need in your life. Therefore, many times he doesn't give you a choice in your relationships. Think about how different children and parents are and how they have no choice in their relationships, and you'll see what I mean. But that lack of smoothly meshing personalities or easy compatibility does not mean you cannot enjoy deep connections with each other. The way you do so is to recognize God's involvement in putting you in those relationships.

My daughter was really unhappy with a certain decision that Sally and I had made. In attempting to get us to change our minds, she referred to her girlfriend's situation by telling us, "But Karen's parents are letting her go!" To this I replied, "I have something hard to say that I don't think you're going to like. When God looked down through history across all the billions of people that there ever were or will be, in all the various times and places where you could have been born, he thought that your mom and I were *the* very best parents that you could ever have." I paused as Cass's eyes clearly registered doubt and disbelief at what she considered a pretty unlikely statement.

I continued, "I didn't say we were the best parents that ever have been. In fact, I know that we are not the best parents in this neighborhood or even on this street. But God thought that we were the very best ones for you. And that means you are the very best child we could ever have. It doesn't do me any good to wish that Karen lived in this family because God didn't think that would be good for Karen or for Mom or for me. We needed you . . . and you needed us."

That recognition softened our interaction. I wasn't approaching her like she was a stubborn problem to be dealt with so I could move on to a hassle-free evening. Instead, both she and I agreed that she's a necessary part of my life just like I'm necessary to her. Recognizing God's sovereign decision in putting this relationship together changes the way I approach her. I was able to stick with the decision my wife and I had made (that Cass still wasn't thrilled about) without it creating friction in our relationship.

The same is true of many of our other relationships. God sovereignly chooses to put you with coworkers and neighbors and in churches where you don't get to choose the personalities around you. He does that because he believes those combinations of people will help shape his kingdom in the way he wants, which in turn will help shape *you*. Your job is to ask how you and they fit into the overall scope of what he is doing.

Our pastor of arts and worship helped me understand what it means to embrace the larger circle of people that God puts into our world. He talked about how worship has to be shaped by the gifts and talents that God in his sovereign, divine providence has brought together, rather than being driven by what someone thinks would be really cool on Sunday. For instance, if God gifts you with people who long to worship and they just happen to be pretty good at playing the banjo, harmonica, and fiddle, then your worship ministry will take on a bluegrass feel. But if God gifts you with three world-class ballerinas, it doesn't matter how much you want bluegrass or how comfortable you feel with that style, that is not the gift-set that God in *his* wisdom and grace has deemed fit to send you at this time.

In other words, God reserves the right to put you in relationships that he thinks will best serve the cause of his glory. Your job is to humbly value and appreciate the people he sends your way.

Sometimes that's hard to do, isn't it? I think many of us get stuck in eighth grade. We're a little more refined now, so at least we've stopped saying, "He's weird!" or "She talks funny, dresses strange, and hangs out with dweebs." But we still use the uncomfortable things people do as an excuse to distance ourselves from them.

Younger people know this is especially hard because they are trying to figure out who they are, what they like, and who likes them. That makes it easy to zero in on the things they don't like about someone and use that to keep their distance from them.

But older folks know this is hard at any age. Don't you still find yourself shying away from people because they don't fit the mold of who you want to be with? Are there people whose phone calls you don't return quite as quickly as someone else's? People who, for some reason, it never occurs to you to invite to your house? You may have graduated middle school, but take a moment and ask yourself if your attitude got held back.

Maybe this will help when you feel yourself shy away from someone God has put you in relationship with. Think about the differences you see between yourself and the other person—whether they are social, economic, cultural, intellectual, educational, or something else. Then take the distance you think separates you from the other person and compare it to the gap that exists between you and Jesus on the same items—social, cultural, intellectual, and so on.

> If you struggle to love someone, or even like *her*, start by asking "What does Jesus enjoy about this person? What traits, strengths, and qualities did he put in her?"

Guess what? Compared to how far both of you are from Jesus, you're virtually at the same place with each other. And if Jesus can be happy with *you* in his family, if he can genuinely appreciate and enjoy *you,* then you can certainly find something to appreciate and enjoy about the other person.

If you struggle to love someone, or even *like* her, start by asking "What does Jesus enjoy about this person? What traits, strengths, and qualities did he put in her?" Keep going. If she's one of his friends then focus on her love for Jesus. How does it affect you when you see her loving the Lord? How does her love for Jesus drive her to care well for others in the same way Jesus does?

Go beyond the externals—go to the heart of the person. If you see her love for Christ, then you will see it expressed for his people. Seeing her heart will affect you, and you'll find yourself drawn to her in love, which will form a more positive context for your relationship.

The Gospel Redefines Friendship

So, if love for Jesus and trust in God's sovereignty defines the core of your relationships, how does it shape the character of those friendships? You can learn a lot about what traits are important in gospel-driven relationships by noticing what Paul says about his friends. Rifle through the pages of your New Testament epistles sometime and single out the references Paul makes to individuals at the beginning or closing of his letters. Then use a concordance to see what else you can learn about them. This won't take long, but will help you understand the kinds of things you should look for in your own friendships.

Not once will you find him saying, "I just love Aurelius! He is an amazing golfer who tells the most outrageous stories! We always have a blast together." Or, "Daphne always looks great and we love getting together for a shopping spree on the weekends. Afterward we grab a couple of lattes and just spend the afternoon catching up. She's so easy to talk to I could hang out with her for hours!"

You see, the gospel redefines relationships and friendships, just like it redefines every other aspect of your life. Paul recognizes he has lots of friends. But the defining aspect of those relationships is not that they are all terrifically wonderful people who think and act just like him. Nor does he tell you they just all get along great and love exactly the same things.

In fact, when you study what he says about his friends you have no idea what they look like, act like in social settings, or do in their spare time. Instead, you learn that they are his partners in the gospel as he and they work for the sake of Christ's people who continue to live in a dark and dangerous world. Here are a few of the character traits Paul honors in his friends (things that should be high on your list of what to look for in your own friendships):

- Paul refers to many people simply as generic "workers in Christ." In Paul's mind—and God's—expending yourself on behalf of God's people is an important part of being a partner. You don't know exactly what they've done, but it's clear that Mary (Romans 16:6), Tryphaena, Tryphosa, Persis (Romans 16:12), Euodia, Syntyche, and Clement (Philippians 4:2–3) have labored for the family of God. That effort is enough for Paul to remember them and respect them.

- He highlights Phoebe's way of loving others by noting that she has provided for many people's physical needs, including Paul's (Romans 16:1–2).

- Similarly Paul values the way his friend Epaphroditus cared for his needs when he was sent by the Philippians (Philippians 2:25), and how Stephanas, Fortunatus, and Achaicus refreshed his spirit (1 Corinthians 16:18).

- He gives special recognition to people like Priscilla, Aquila (Acts 18:26), and Timothy (1 Corinthians 4:17; 2 Corinthians 1:19), who built up the family of Christ through their teaching ministry.

- Other friends helped Paul to love the church by writing letters—some as ghostwriters (Tertius in Romans 16:22), but even more as authors. When you talk about "the Pauline epistles" it is easy to forget that *Timothy* gets coauthor credit for the letters of 2 Corinthians, Philippians, Colossians, 1 and 2 Thessalonians, and Philemon. Nor is it often remembered that *Silvanus* is part of the "we" who speak throughout 1 and 2 Thessalonians, where the first person singular "I" is rarely used. *Luke* not only faithfully chronicled Paul's trips in the book of Acts, but his presence is enough to turn a third-person narrative about Paul into the first-person "we" midway through the book.

- Tychicus, the beloved brother and faithful minister of Ephesians (6:21–22) partnered in the gospel by keeping Paul's friends informed of how Jesus' other friends were doing. Among all the things that Tychicus did in his life, that's the only thing we know about him. If you look up the five times that his name appears in our New Testament, you'll discover that each time he is either traveling or being sent somewhere by Paul. Can you imagine setting aside a line item in the church budget to fund his ministry? God can. This is such an important aspect of gospel-centered care for each other that Paul had a guy dedicated to being a living newsletter.

- Another important way people partnered with Paul was through their prayers. He relied on other people for spiritual and physical deliverance (Romans 15:30; 2 Corinthians 1:11; Philippians 1:19; and Philemon 22). Even more amazing is his request that the Ephesians pray for him so that words may be given to him for boldly opening his mouth to proclaim the mystery of the gospel (Ephesians 6:18–20).

  Think about this for a moment: Paul—the *apostle* Paul—who saw the risen Christ. Paul—*the* missionary without compare. Paul—who builds the church. *This* Paul asks for prayer. Even though he is the apostle to the Gentiles, he doesn't think he's above them and has no need of their help. In essence he says, "I can't do the job God has given me without you. I need to have words given to me or I will not be able to help people see and grasp the gospel for their own lives." He asks for their partnership in order to carry out the ministry God has given him.

- The more generic word "partner" (as in 2 Corinthians 8:23; Philippians 1:5; and Philemon 17) expands in the book of Philippians to include "fellow workers" (2:25; 4:3), side-by-side laborers (Philippians 4:3), "fellow soldier" (Philippians 2:25; see also Philemon 2), and a "true companion" who Paul believes can help resolve an ongoing dispute (Philippians 4:3). Are you getting a taste of how much deeper than merely being friends this gospel partnering goes?

A Community of Co-Laborers

Paul doesn't live out his faith as an isolated, Lone Ranger individual. He's surrounded by relationships—friends who partner together in their love for Christ and for his kingdom. He serves with people who were drawn to each other because Jesus first drew them to himself.

It is this sense of joint ownership, of being co-laborers as part of a larger team, that I have really enjoyed as I transitioned from working in a stand-alone counseling center to working within a church. From the earliest moments other staff members wanted to know how the people I counseled were doing. They were not inappropriately nosy, but they had referred people to me and were checking to see if those people were being helped. Suddenly I was accountable to peers in a way that I hadn't been before, which was both good for me and the people I counseled. But even better, I was serving alongside others who could provide more resources than I ever could on my own.

That sense of shared responsibility for each other is what we try to promote in our support groups. There people experience relationships that begin with a shared experience or struggle, but quickly grow to helping each other as they wrestle with their lives. I can't tell you how exciting it has been to watch guys in our sexual purity group openly discuss things that they formerly wouldn't have whispered in the dark.

They don't do so to brag, but to invite input from each other and learn how to give wise counsel to each other. I was amazed one night as I watched four of my brothers coach another man about which resource would best help him prepare for a conversation he needed to initiate with his wife. And it's not all one-sided either. At the following meeting, the same man led the group as we tried to help a different brother see where he was dangerously deceiving himself.

In the fullest sense of the word, these guys are partners with each other in the gospel. They would not naturally have sought each other out, given their very different personalities and backgrounds. But underneath all of their surface differences, they have forged a fellowship so deep that when we merged two groups a year later, one man would introduce his group by saying, "These are my best friends."

Their friendship is not based on external similarities. But like the disciples before them, they know that Jesus has shared with them everything he'd heard from his Father. They in turn share those things with each other. Their friendship with Jesus gives them a deep friendship with each other.

On Your Own

1. What have you normally thought of as the most important qualities to look for in a friend? How does Jesus' desire to be friends with you affect your list?

2. How does the way you complement your friends (and vice versa) help people see Jesus better?

3. Who are the people you struggle to befriend? Who in your world turns you off? Spend some time realizing how, from God's perspective, the two of you are more alike than different.

4. What makes you a difficult person for others to befriend? Where does God call you to change for the sake of building stronger relationships with the different people he has placed you with?

CHAPTER 7

Pursuing Love:
Shepherding Each Other

People stray. They stray from what is good for them and, often simultaneously, they stray from relationships that would help them. When the people in your life put themselves in that kind of danger, you need to gently go after them to urge them back to what is good and healthy. This chapter looks at that kind of love—pursuing love.

God is good at pursuing you, even when you're already one of his friends. One of the predominant metaphors he uses to describe his relationship with you is the image of a shepherd, of someone who carefully watches over his sheep to make sure they don't set themselves up to get hurt. He notices when his friends wander off, but then he goes out of his way to find them and bring them back to a safe place.

Pursuing love is far different than a heavy-handed accountability or a detective-like invasion of someone else's life. Pursuing love makes sure people know that you want what is best for them even when they don't. If you want to communicate to your friends "I long for what is best for you," then you need to develop your ability to pursue them for their benefit.

Ryan, the coleader of our support group walked in one night, said hi, and asked if I thought he should call Keith. Keith had left him a voicemail a little earlier complaining of a long day at work in the heat that resulted in a headache. He said he was going to skip the meeting that night and just take it easy. If Keith had called me, I would have accepted what he said and not given it a second thought.

But Ryan knew better. He flipped open his phone and called. "Hey, man, we need you. We've got food. We've got AC. We can help with your headache. It'd be great to see you, even if you get here a bit late. Why don't you come?" I stood there hardly daring to believe what I was hearing.

Ryan knew all about straying sheep. In his own self-absorption he had nearly destroyed his marriage just a few years earlier. Yet here he was, reaching out to another of God's precious children. It was an amazing moment to see grace in action.

And that was exactly what Keith needed. He showed up later that evening. And it was good—both for him and for us. He needed to be with his brothers, but he needed to be pursued so a brother sought him out. One formerly lost sheep diligently pursuing another because he knew something about straying sheep: they need to be pursued.

Jesus' Heart for His People

Ryan learned from Jesus, who is the first to know that straying sheep need to be pursued. In Luke 15 he tells three parables that describe his heart and the heart of his Father for those who have lost their way. He is a shepherd who leaves ninety-nine sheep who are doing fine in order to pursue one that is in trouble. He pictures himself as a woman who loses one of her precious coins, then lights a lamp, sweeps the house, and searches diligently until she finds it. Or you can imagine a heartbroken father who abandons his dignity by racing down the road to embrace a smelly, destitute son who formerly was interested only in taking him for all he was worth.

I used to think of these passages primarily as evangelistic. You know, "This is how God pursues non-Christians." The reality is that this describes God's heart and attitude in general for people, including those already in his family.

Think with me about Psalm 119. You might already know that this is the longest psalm in the Bible. For 175 verses the songwriter focuses on the goodness of God's Word and how his voice is something his people long for with all their hearts. Finally he wraps everything up in one resounding conclusion, leaving your mind as you walk away from the psalm fixed on the words "I have strayed like a lost sheep. Seek your servant, for I have not forgotten your commands" (Psalm 119:176, NIV).

"I have strayed like a lost sheep." Who are God's people? We are those who stray. Even as a redeemed person, part of your nature is that you wander from what you know is true, right, and good. That's part of your identity as a fallen creature. But that's not all— otherwise your life would be hopeless. Your hope is that you're in a relationship with someone who understands your nature, someone to whom you can cry out to come looking for you: "Lord, seek your servant!" Jesus uses this picture when he describes his own heart in Luke 15. He is this kind of shepherd who looks for you when you fail.

Now perhaps you already believe you have a shepherd who looks for you when you sin, but the shepherd in your mind is not a good shepherd. He grumbles about how much trouble you're causing him, how he hates looking for you in the dark, or how it'll be your fault if he twists his ankle among the rocks where you're stuck. He wonders out loud if you're worth it. And he lets you know you had better not get lost again or he might let you stay out there, because that'll teach you a good lesson. You can almost hear him say, "When I find you, you're going to be sorry!"

Jesus isn't like that. He calls himself the good shepherd, someone who is not simply a hired hand with no concern for the flock. Because the flock is his own, he's willing to give everything he has for them, even if that means his very life (John 10:11–12).

"Shepherd" is a great word to describe God's heart for his people. Micah prophesied that out of Bethlehem would come a *ruler* who would *shepherd* God's people (Micah 5:2–4; see also Matthew 2:6). That's a difficult combination to pull off. Not a harsh overlord, but one who tends to both the needs and protection of the people. Micah makes it clear that people will live securely under this kind of ruling care.

Jesus chose the image of a shepherd to illustrate the relationship between himself and his people. He felt compassion for the crowds because they were harassed and helpless; they were like sheep without a shepherd. And he was not okay with that. Because they lacked shepherds, Jesus not only urged his disciples to pray that God would send more workers to help, he sent out the twelve apostles as well (Matthew 9:36–10:4). He looks for people who will shepherd like he himself does.

Maybe you can think of someone who is close to you right now who needs a shepherd. I know I can. A child who seems to set himself against you by constantly testing everything you say. A formerly close friend whose new boyfriend doesn't seem to be a good influence on her and seems to be pulling her away from her other friends. A parent who is becoming more difficult as age destroys his mental and physical abilities. A neighbor you haven't seen for the past few weeks of February who has a history of being depressed during the dark winter months.

If you consider the people you know, you will quickly realize there is at least one person who needs someone to pursue him or her. The difficulty is not in finding straying sheep. It's in finding true shepherds.

God's Call to Shepherds

Sadly, the lack of genuine shepherds Jesus noted went back years before he was born. Israel's shepherds had a history of caring more for themselves than for those in their care.

> The word of the LORD came to me: "Son of man, prophesy against the shepherds of Israel; prophesy, and say to them, even to the shepherds, Thus says the LORD GOD: Ah, shepherds of Israel who have been feeding yourselves! Should not shepherds feed the sheep? You eat the fat, you clothe yourselves with the wool, you slaughter the fat ones, but you do not feed the sheep." (Ezekiel 34:1–3)

God rebukes the bad shepherds of Israel. While they enjoyed the material benefits of being in charge of the sheep, they had not taken care of the flock that God had entrusted to them. The chapter is a strong, frightening indictment against them. You do not want to be on the receiving end of this passage.

Read it in reverse, however, and you catch a beautiful glimpse of God's heart that shows how he cares for his sheep that are not doing well.

> "The weak you have not strengthened, the sick you have not healed, the injured you have not bound up, the strayed you have not brought back, the lost you have not sought, and with force and harshness you have ruled them." (Ezekiel 34:4)

Flip those phrases around and notice what God tells you about the kinds of people a shepherd serves and how he wants shepherds to care for them. He wants shepherds who will strengthen the weak, heal the sick, bind up the injured, bring back the strays, seek the lost, and gently guide the sheep.

Do you see God's gracious attitude toward those who are in trouble? He wants shepherds who will give themselves to the work of building up and pursuing people who are damaged and lost—even when that damage is self-inflicted. He wants shepherds who actively pursue the hurting sheep in order to nurse them back to health.

This is a very warm, inviting look into God's heart for his people. Wouldn't you want to be in a community where the shepherds lived out those things? It's a wonderful passage.

It's also a troubling passage. Who can consistently love this way? Weak, sick, and straying people are not nice to be around. They refuse to help themselves. They misread your motives, they resist your attempts to help, and they run away. Who can keep giving them the kind of help they need? You can't and I can't.

> He wants shepherds who will give themselves to the work of building up and pursuing people who are damaged and lost—even when that damage is self-inflicted. He wants shepherds who actively pursue the hurting sheep in order to nurse them back to health.

God Shepherds You First

I remember one bedtime when my son was not getting himself ready for bed nearly fast enough to please me. You know how these things go. For some reason I began equating how quickly he moved with how much he respected me—and I found him grossly wanting. The more I demanded immediate action, the more I interpreted any slowness from him as an intentional slap in my face.

Each time I tried to move him along, I got louder. I became increasingly critical. There was less he could do right and more he was doing wrong. As most exchanges like that go, it ended badly, with me losing my temper and loudly demanding that he get in bed immediately.

He left, but do you know there's something worse than being in a room with someone who is making you crazy? It's being left alone in a room with your conscience and with the Holy Spirit after you've just sinned against someone. There is nowhere to go and no one else you can blame for your own bad actions. Now you have to deal with yourself.

I picked up my Bible and started reading Ezekiel 34 because I knew I had shepherded badly. I could not have chosen a better passage. I managed to get only to verse 2 before conviction really took hold. Here I am, charged with shepherding and protecting my family, and all I care about is whether my son makes my life easier or harder.

Reading further simply strengthened the conviction, especially as I read, "You have ruled them harshly and brutally" (NIV). That was true of me! Written thousands of years ago, the Word of God spoke directly to what I had just done. There was no denying it, so I confessed my sin to the Lord and asked him to meet me in the middle of my failure.

He did. As you continue reading the passage, you realize that no human shepherd can ever provide what God longs for his people to experience. But he cares too much for his people to leave them without a shepherd so he planned to become the supreme shepherd who was and is exactly what his people need.

> "For thus says the LORD GOD: Behold, I, I myself will search for my sheep and will seek them out. As a shepherd seeks out his flock when he is among his sheep that have been scattered, so

will I seek out my sheep, and I will rescue them from all places where they have been scattered on a day of clouds and thick darkness. . . . I myself will be the shepherd of my sheep, and I myself will make them lie down, declares the LORD GOD. I will seek the lost, and I will bring back the strayed, and I will bind up the injured, and I will strengthen the weak, and the fat and the strong I will destroy. I will feed them in justice. . . . I will rescue my flock; they shall no longer be a prey. And I will judge between sheep and sheep. And I will set up over them one shepherd, my servant David, and he shall feed them: he shall feed them and be their shepherd." (Ezekiel 34:11–12; 15–16; 22–23)

In that moment, as I sat reading on the couch, his Spirit spoke to me, making me realize that *he* is not like the earlier shepherds he talked about. He is a good shepherd who does not rule his flock harshly or brutally. And that means he doesn't rule me harshly— even when I've been harsh with others. Right there, in my living room, after having just sinned against my little boy, there is still a shepherd for me who will seek me out when I've strayed.

Obviously that doesn't mean I take lightly what I've done. He is, after all, convicting me strongly of my sin. But he is not harsh in his conviction, and he doesn't destroy me. In fact, he has already taken my sin on himself and dealt with it. I am free from guilt (though I may not be free from the effect of what I've just done). Having been forgiven was a wonderful thing that resulted in me going to my son and asking his forgiveness. Having a good shepherd come looking for me moved me closer to my God. It also restored me to being the shepherd I'm supposed to be so that I could go looking for my own straying sheep.

My failure was the context for once again experiencing the love of God, but in such a way that I hated my sin and hated what I'd done both to my son and to my God. When God seeks you out, you move closer to him. As you become more intimate with him, your life more closely mirrors his.

You will fail as an under-shepherd. But when you fail, remember that you have a shepherd too. He pursues you so you can again take the responsibility he calls you to. And when you have experienced his shepherding, you become more like the kind of shepherd he is. You seek out those who are straying in order to bring them back.

That is the crying need of our relationships today—that we would know how to pursue those who have strayed. It's the need of our families and our friends. It's the need of our small group relationships and, from where I sit during the week as a pastor, it's the desperate need of our churches.

What Pursuit Is Not

Before we consider what it looks like to helpfully pursue someone, let's think first about what pursuit is not. I know of one woman who, in the middle of her crumbling marriage, received a four-page letter from her church stating its theological position on when and how divorce was acceptable. They intended that impersonal document to minister to her in her situation. It was about as helpful as the phone call another lady received from the pastor of the church she had stopped attending some months earlier. He launched into a monologue that ran for nearly half an hour along the general theme of why the decisions she was making were all wrong.

Or consider the guidance one board of elders received as they discussed a pastoral situation. A woman from their congregation had developed the habit of going to clubs, getting picked up, and then sleeping around. In reviewing the church governance manual they learned that they were supposed to send her a certified letter summoning her to appear before the church court of the elders. In disbelief, one of the elders exploded, "Might as well send her a letter saying, 'Go away and never come back!' " Another responded by saying, "We need to call her—go to her house—do whatever it takes to contact her personally."

Those brothers understood that the spirit of Christ's pursuit does not consist of a distant ultimatum, impersonal information, or a noninteractive proclamation. Instead, it involves you personally stepping outside your comfort zone to help another reconnect relationally with Christ and his people.

Pursuit is also not based on my own neediness. I do not pursue you because I have a deep, unmet need that you will fill if you return. I don't pursue you because that will let me have you in my life. I don't pursue you because, in return, you will make my life easier. I don't pursue you because that will mean I no longer need to stay up all night worrying about where you are, what you're doing, and with whom you're doing it. And I especially don't pursue you because that will make me feel good about myself—as though I have worth and value because I have come after you to help keep you from ruining your life.

In other words, if I successfully pursue you in a godly way, then I am not the one who will benefit the most. You will. If that's not the case, then I'm not really pursuing *you*. Instead, I'm pursuing you because doing so will get me something that I long for. You become a means to an end for me. That's very similar to Tasha's experience when a friend helped her see that she served others primarily so that she could feel needed by them. It is too easy to run after someone simply because the experience gives you what you want.

Seeking someone is also not the same as chasing him. If, in moving toward someone, he moves further away, then he doesn't want godliness; what he wants is a safety net. He wants to know that someone cares—but he's not interested in real help. That is not what seeking a stray is about.

What Pursuit Is

Pursuing your friend comes from a heart that says "You are in trouble and you matter to me." You try to help her realize that what she is doing will damage her if she does not stop, turn around, and go in a different direction. So you find ways to let her know what you see and where you think she will end up if she keeps going. You let her know that you care about what she is doing to herself. You also give her the opportunity of seeing how she is affecting you. You avoid manipulating her, but you talk openly about how what she does grieves or angers or scares you.

> *Pursuing your friend comes from a heart that says "You are in trouble and you matter to me."*

You let your son see you weep when he responds to your rebuke with the stony look on his face that reflects the hardness of his heart. You let your daughter know your concerns that she cares more about what her friends think than what her Lord does. You reach out to your friend who seems to indulge his appetites with greater frequency as the years go by, looking more for comfort in what he eats and drinks or views than in his God. Lost sheep need to know they matter enough to you that you'll come looking for them to let them know what you see.

Second, you let people know not only that they *can* come back, but that you *want* them back. You find a million different ways to say "You are welcome here. I want back what we had," or even, "I want something better with you than we've ever had!"

Straying people struggle to believe they're wanted. Deep conviction feels like wearing a heavy coat of shame. People in that condition need to know there are wide open, welcoming arms longing to embrace them—literally, not just figuratively. Pursuing them means letting them know how much you want their friendship.

My daughter knew deep shame. She hated what she had done and wanted nothing more to do with it, but she also keenly felt the embarrassment of it. More than that, though, she feared how it would affect her relationship with me. She cried to my wife, "This is going to ruin my friendship with Daddy." And so, being fearful of how I would respond, she tried to avoid me. Her fear drove her to protect herself.

Keeping in mind this shepherding God, I reached out to hug her, but she responded with a cold, rigid side hug. Have you ever tried to hug someone who doesn't hug back? You get all the relational connection of hugging a telephone pole.

I wasn't satisfied with that so I said, "No, come here." Then we had a full, warm hug, including tears, which resulted in full restoration. She knew that because I loved her I was not about to settle for a broken relationship with her.

Now, I'm no saint (just ask my daughter about other times), but I do have a God who rushes to find sinners just so he can pardon them and restore what they've destroyed. I don't have a God who sinfully scolds, explodes, or is critical. Instead, I have this Jesus who reaches out to me in my unworthiness to welcome me back. And, in turn, I try to pass on that same welcome.

Third, part of pursuing well involves helping the person realize he needs to respond to being sought. When Jesus seeks out strays, he lets them know that there is a free offer for them to experience a better, deeper, richer life—and they need to want that life. They need to return.

It's a little like proactively introducing a cease-fire in a battle, during which time you drop care packages on the enemy. Each package comes with a note that offers additional aid and comfort for anyone who will lay down his arms and rebellion against the king and join his community. The package is a taste of the greater goodness that could be his, but he must respond to it in order to receive a larger helping. He cannot expect to keep receiving aid if he is unwilling to receive the king.

When you seek out someone who is straying, you are offering

her a taste of grace that attempts to woo her back to her rightful shepherd and to the sheepfold. Seeking comes with the implication that she needs to come back.

By now you probably realize that pursuing people well is not a cookie-cutter, one-size-fits-all activity. It looks and sounds differently depending on the person involved. A scared person doesn't need (and can't use) the same message that a stubborn or confused or hurt person needs. That means wise shepherds must carefully consider the person involved and assess what she needs to hear.

Types of Pursuit

Shepherds also have to assess what kind of pursuit is needed. There are the times when you need to pursue someone who is actively running away. My lead pastor is especially good at this kind of pursuit. One young man has talked about the voicemails, e-mails, and text messages the pastor sent him during the years when he acted out the part of the prodigal son.

Small things? No way. Although the messages may have been brief, his reaching out indicated that those straying are important to him, that he's concerned, and that there is a place for them to return when they're sick of being trapped by what they're doing. People who actively run need to know that someone cares about them.

Not everyone who strays does so actively or intentionally. Sometimes you have to pursue people who *passively* fall off your radar. People do that. They're not in immediate trouble or danger, and so, in a hectic, crisis-driven world, you easily forget that they too have needs. While it's true that the squeaky wheel gets the grease, the silent, forgotten wheels often become squeaky through neglect.

One of the things I've learned to do is make myself consciously think about who I've been passing over. Those are the people I need to make a special effort to reconnect with. I do this most regularly with my children. I'll take time to think about each one and ask myself, *When was the last time I spent time doing something just with him or her?* Invariably someone is at the bottom of the list. We've said good morning to each other, seen each other in passing, and caught up about our days, but I haven't made special time just to be with that one.

So I make myself take time to think about what that person likes to do. I want to invite this child to spend time with me so the activity needs to be inviting to him or her, not just to me. Then when I get home I'll pull that one aside and ask, "Later tonight, would you like to _____ (fill in the blank: play a game, take a walk, read a book, build your model, sit out back and talk, throw a ball, cook something together, or do something special.)?" I can't guarantee he or she will take me up on my offer, but I can invite this special person not to fall off the radar.

While I was writing this I paused to take a phone call. The call was from a man I served with to lead a small group. He was just driving through the area on business when my name came to his mind so, since we haven't connected recently, he called. There was nothing on his mind. It was just a five-minute phone call to reestablish a relationship that had been idling—falling off the radar. He didn't merely have the thought and then dismiss it because he was too busy; he acted on it for the sake of the relationship.

Another intentional way I pursue people is by building them in to my schedule. These are times when there isn't a problem or even a potential problem. But since maintaining relationships is one of the best ways to prevent straying, we decide to do something that brings us together. I have several close friendships where we have mutually decided to put ourselves on each other's calendars—every other week or once a month—simply to share our lives with each other.

On a daily basis in my home, this is dinnertime. It's a nearly nonnegotiable time when the family all comes together. We don't watch TV, answer the phone, or allow books or toys at the table. Instead, it's a time to reconnect after being out of the house all day, separated from each other.

You can also schedule less frequent times on a regular basis, such as a family fun night or a weekly date night. Following a friend's example, I've built in a weekly breakfast date with my kids. I take a different child each week to the local diner before school to be together, have fun, and share our lives. I can't tell you how many great conversations we've had about what's taking place in my life and in theirs or about what we need to think about for the future. The fact that each kid keeps track of whose week it is to go testifies to the goodness of those times even when there isn't a great conversation.

Pursuing people is more than simply waiting to bump into someone. It's more than just finding people when there's a problem. It is careful, regular attention. It's a lot like watering plants.

A friend of mine has killed every plant ever placed in her care. Plants need regular attention. If you ignore them for days (or weeks!) at a time, they will die. Flooding a bone-dry, withered plant with water is not the kind of attention it needs to thrive. That's crisis intervention, which is not the same as regular, intentional, thoughtful care. People need even more proactive, regular attention than plants do to grow up in healthy ways. That means you must regularly involve yourself in their lives.

Pursuing people means you actively look for them because they need to know you love them and want what's best for them. By going after them you communicate that they are wanted and valued. Even when they've made a mess of their lives, you reach out to them to let them know that you love them too much to leave them alone in their mess. You go after them, just like Jesus goes after you.

On Your Own

1. What keeps you from pursuing others? Is it too much trouble? Are you afraid that they'll lash out? Or maybe you're angry that you have to go after them one more time. Think carefully about the reasons you give yourself as to why you don't go after other people when they stray.

2. How many times has Jesus pursued you?

3. When was the last time you were aware of his pursuit? What was that experience like for you? Think about what it was like before, during, and after he came looking for you.

4. Do you have a friend or acquaintance who needs you to search for them? Make sure you ask Jesus to bring to your mind people you may forget or even ignore. How do you need to approach them?

CHAPTER 8

Communicating Love:
Talking with Each Other

Another aspect of loving well that creates a context for relationships to flourish is communicating love. The simple act of talking is underrated as a primary means for growing healthy relationships. So much of how we mature and thrive comes through communicating our thoughts and ideas to each other. Strong human relationships are characterized by regular, meaningful dialogue just like you find within the divine community. This chapter explores communicating love.

The prominence that conversation needs to have in your relationships grows directly out of how important it is to the members of the Trinity that they communicate with each other and with you. Our God is not silent in his relationships with you, and neither can you be with others.

Unfortunately, conversation is one of the first things to disappear when a relationship is difficult. Most every married couple who has come to me for counseling has cited communication as a problem area between them that they want to change. Sometimes one spouse believes he's heard everything the other has to say and so he thinks, *What's the point of hearing it again?* Or she becomes convinced that it doesn't matter what she says because he doesn't seem to be listening. Either way, they talk less and less, until they become used to not talking with each other. The same dynamic happens between parents with their children and between friends who grow estranged.

> ... before we can develop healthy patterns of communication, we must first regain a sense of its glory.

This may seem like an odd place to begin, but before we can develop healthy patterns of communication, we must first regain a sense of its glory. Surrounded daily as we are by words, we treat them as necessary means to an end, growing dull to the wonder of what's taking place as two lives interpenetrate each other through language.

Communication as a Window into Glory

My cat chirps. It's kind of a trill that lasts less than a second. Very cute. Very endearing. Nearly impossible to understand. Sometimes it means he's hungry. Sometimes it means he wants to be noticed. But most of the time, I have no idea what he wants. So he wanders around the house chirping.

My daughter doesn't chirp. I came out of my office one morning about a decade ago when she was somewhere between one and two years old and sitting in her high chair. I bent down, kissed her on the head, and pronounced her, "Kissable"—a benediction that I had never before given anywhere to anyone. Smiling, Cassie immediately responded with her own never-before-heard request, "More kissable."

That's remarkable. She attached meaning to a word that was new to her and to our household, correctly understanding my intent in the way I used the word. Then without hesitating she gave the word back to me, along with her own additions, in order to express her desire, fully expecting me to understand her—even though no one in my 30-plus years of life experience at the time had ever used that combination with me before. And I did understand her. Laughing, I kissed her again, bringing bigger smiles to her face.

It happened so quickly and felt so ordinary, but slow it down and it is glorious. That two completely distinct individuals could pass thoughts, beliefs, attitudes, feelings, and requests to each other in a matter of seconds and be completely understood by each other is something that should cause us to pause and worship every single time it happens. There is a dim shadow of something divine taking place in a three-second interaction with a toddler that doesn't happen anywhere in the rest of creation. It is a thing to be marveled at, not taken for granted or treated as mundane.

That I am able to make sense of the things I experience in life, reflect on them, and use them to inform what I do next is a testimony to the image of God in an *individual*. But to share that information with you in a form that makes sense to you and for you to receive it—even though you have your own thought processes, understandings of the world, and experiences—is a testimony to the image of God in *community*. It is a God-thing that only exists when we are with each other.

God's Commitment to Conversation

God loves talking within himself. Each member of the Trinity is in constant, regular communication with the other two. You catch snatches of this conversation in the Old Testament even before the full-blown revelation that three persons share the one essence of our God (Genesis 1:26–27; 3:22; Psalm 2:7; 110:1). Those scraps of conversation hint at an ongoing deep and rich relationship whose contours come into focus in the gospels.

Jesus actively relates to his Father, spending long times with him (Luke 5:16; 6:12; 9:28), both talking (John 11:41–42) and listening (John 5:19–20). The Holy Spirit also "talks" as he leads Jesus into the wilderness (Mark 1:12) or listens so he can later tell Jesus' friends what he has heard (John 14:26; 16:13; 1 Corinthians 2:9–10). It becomes clearer that an extended conversation takes place within the godhead as the author of Hebrews strings together several instances of it (Hebrews 1:5, 8–13).

Not only is he conversing, but in God's opinion the conversation is just too good to miss, so he creates others to share it with. He talks to his friends. Adam, Noah, Abraham, Moses, Joshua, and David all come quickly to mind.

Sadly, humans, including God's family, aren't very good at communicating in a divine manner. Blame-shifting, half-truths, full-blown lies, insults, sarcasm, criticism, condescension, groveling, complaining, slandering—the ways we hurt each other with our words are as varied as our personalities. It seems that the more potential a human characteristic has to display the glory of God, the greater power it has to hurt and destroy when it is twisted. Instead of reflecting God with the way we use our words, we too often portray the deceiver.

> Instead of reflecting God with the way we use our words, we too often portray the deceiver.

How does God deal with people who wander far from him by using his wonderful gift of speech to tear down and plot against each other? He talks to them. He pleads with his people, warns them, instructs them, and pours out his heart to them. Conversation is one of the primary ways he expresses his love for people. Yes, there is a point where judgment comes and the time for talking ends, but wow, can you imagine simply talking anywhere near as long or as often as he does? In my own relationships, I am tempted to quit talking a lot sooner than he is.

My daughter and I were riding in the car when I said, "Cassie, put your feet down, you're getting my car seat dirty." Several minutes went by and the feet returned. "Honey, this is why I get frustrated because my words don't seem to make a difference in your life."

My girl endured my lecture with an appropriate, penitential bowed head. Then the feet returned. "Don't you realize this is why some people yell at their kids? I'm kinder, but you're taking advantage of my kindness and yelling is starting to look attractive to me. At least it would keep my seats clean!" And lose my daughter—oh, right. That.

A few more minutes and the feet start sliding back up. But then a curious thing happened. Before I could say anything, a course correction happened and her legs crossed rather than continuing upward. She did hear me. My words did matter, but man, you have to talk. After only three attempts I was ready to throw in the towel—and I got results. What was it like for God as he talked for hundreds of years with little to no response?

Flip through the various historical and prophetic books of the Old Testament and notice how often God talked to his people when they were straying. Can you count how many times you come across the phrase, "The word of the Lord came to _____, the prophet"? Notice his commitment to a conversation. His willingness to try again. His persistence.

I would have given up long before he did. For all his trouble he got ignored and rejected, yet he kept talking—not because he was needy, but because *they* were. He kept up that steady, persistent rhythm of the Word of the Lord coming to people over hundreds of years, finally culminating in Jesus.

Jesus was not the stereotypical strong and silent type, limiting himself to 7,000 words per day. He talked all the time. He was constantly teaching, preaching, comforting, rebuking, encouraging, and telling stories. Clearly, he didn't talk just to hear the sound of his own voice, nor was he a babbling brook that meandered endlessly. Rather, he spoke with a purpose, driven by his passion that people would know his Father and be drawn into his kingdom. Little wonder that John in his Gospel seizes on him as the Word of God become flesh. Jesus was *the* speaker, *the* teacher, *the* talker without compare.

We need to be that persistent. Do you have a child whom you don't seem to be getting through to? Maybe a spouse or a friend? As tempting as it may be to quit trying and give up, you can't afford to, not if you really love that person. That doesn't mean you talk nonstop or nag the person, following him through the house. It means you continue to show your relational goodwill by letting the other person know you're longing to have a conversation if and when he is. Keeping a conversation going, or at least available, is the way you express this kind of love in your relationships.

Jada knew Adrian was lying to her . . . again. The evidence was clear in the things he'd left around and in his demeanor toward her. But he wouldn't admit it. That frustrated her. She could handle what he'd done, but being lied to cut away at the core of their relationship. What can you do, however, when the other person won't come clean?

You talk—which she did. Every few days she re-raised the issue—not harping on him, not hurting him, but persisting. She let him know how she felt and gave him opportunities to be honest. He rejected those opportunities for nearly a month, until he was finally convinced that she was safe enough and important enough to reveal what he'd done. She didn't get immediate results, but over time she created a context with her words that invited him to a more meaningful relationship.

Jada is the kind of redeemed talker you will find among Jesus' friends—one who constantly shares her life and faith through the simple activity of talking. As you scan the New Testament examples and commands, you quickly realize how much emphasis God puts on speaking well. Healthy relationships are marked by human conversation extending the conversation God has initiated with his people.

Peter the apostle understood that divinity has broken into our human conversations.

> As each has received a gift, use it to serve one another, as good stewards of God's varied grace: whoever speaks, as one who speaks oracles of God; whoever serves, as one who serves by the strength that God supplies—in order that in everything God may be glorified through Jesus Christ. To him belong glory and dominion forever and ever. Amen. (1 Peter 4:10–11)

Do you take your conversations with others as seriously as God does? When you speak, you are to do so with the conscious awareness that you are speaking God's words. You are part of the ongoing, God-oriented conversation because you are part of his family. Our God likes to talk, and his people do too. Here are a few important ways that conversation should take place with your friends.

Healthy Relationships Never Stop Learning

First, healthy relationships look to give and receive input from one another. From the earliest days of the church, God's people have understood that in a dark world it is essential to be called back regularly to the kind of life that pleases God. And so we look to be taught by others (Acts 2:42; 2 Timothy 2:2). We approach our relationships welcoming godly input and looking to each other to provide it. The flip side of that equation is that we are willing to offer others the things we've learned as well.

I have been so encouraged this past year by what I see among the men in my support group. Men who once walked in embarrassment and defeat over the struggles in their lives learned how to better live their faith. How has that happened? They talk openly about the failures in their lives. And they welcome others into that conversation. They invite each other to give them feedback. They ask questions of each other. They offer answers. Literally, they teach each other.

Each week they discuss the questions they have about how their faith connects—or doesn't connect—with their life. In doing that they are discovering that Jesus really meets them there. Their friendships are marked by serving as mutual learners and teachers.

That's a hard combination to achieve. Typically, our relationships are more one-sided, with one person being "the learner" and one "the teacher." Love that takes communication seriously simultaneously looks to share with others and receive from them. If you want to see your friendships mature, you need to incorporate both of these aspects into your conversations.

Healthy Relationships Gently Confront

Sadly, in a broken world, there are times when your conversation needs to become more pointed to help your friend see things he's not doing well or needs to change.

You have not been brought into a family that ignores problems or sweeps them under the rug. I know that some people have had those kinds of experiences, but God's family is different. Here, when there's something wrong between people, we put things on the table that need to be dealt with. Jesus was very clear: "Pay attention to yourselves! If your brother sins, rebuke him, and if he repents, forgive him" (Luke 17:3). We don't let sin fester.

However, the way this is communicated is really important. When we have these conversations, they're not harsh or destructive. They don't come with raised voices, emotional venting, or blowouts that result in cold, bitter feelings. Rather we are guided by Scriptures like 1 Timothy 5:1–2: "Do not rebuke an older man but encourage him as you would a father. Treat younger men as brothers, older women as mothers, younger women as sisters, in all purity." The New American Standard captures the sense of the phrase even better when it translates it as "Do not sharply rebuke."

Do you hear Paul's concern for gentleness? You don't ignore the problem—you meet it head on. But you do so with patience and kindness, not sharpness or harshness. Loving well insists that you bring a positive connotation to these conversations so that your words are as easy to hear as possible.

One day when he was five years old, my son Timmy came into the living room to find me. He was clearly agitated. He turned his face up to mine and, without a trace of bitterness or anger but with some tightness in his voice, said, "Dad, when you talk to Mom like that, I feel like taking away your cookies!"

Did you hear that? Direct and honest, not nasty or vindictive. He was respectful, but he called it like it was: "This is what you did. Here's how I want to respond (I want to punish you) when you do that. And I don't like the effect you're having on us very much." A simple, yet very clear statement of how hard I can be to live with.

I really needed that moment of ministry from him. I needed to hear how I sounded, but that meant I needed someone to care about the effect I was having on my relationships. Timmy met my need by courageously speaking up to help me see what I was doing. He didn't do it for his benefit. In fact, if you think about it, that was a scary place to put himself if I hadn't been willing to hear him. You take that risk for someone else's sake only when you have his best interests at heart.

Healthy Relationships Encourage

Sometimes you need to help your friends by saying "here is what's true." Other times they need you to say "There seems to be something wrong here." Still another important way you love them is by telling them "Great job—keep going!"

When you encourage the people around you, it gives them confidence to keep going. "The one who prophesies speaks to people for their upbuilding and encouragement and consolation" (1 Corinthians 14:3). In that sense, there's not a lot of difference between the words "encourage" and "exhort." In fact, they are so similar in meaning that they can be used together, as Paul does for the Thessalonians.

> For you know how, like a father with his children, we *exhorted each one of you and encouraged you* and charged you to walk in a manner worthy of God, who calls you into his own kingdom and glory. (1 Thessalonians 2:11–12, emphasis added)

Again, you can't miss the gentleness in the phrase "like a father with his children." He is not harsh, but he is *clearly* concerned that they turn out well.

Encouragement is far more important than we often realize. It's an attitude that focuses more on the reality of what Christians are becoming than on where they are presently failing. You realize that, in the end, every one of God's children will end up pure and perfect because God has taken on himself the burden of purifying us. Then you emphasize where you see hints and glimmers of that future glory pressing itself into the present moment.

Encouragement is much more than a pat on the back. It's inviting someone to become aware of the evidence in her life that shows God is at work. In effect, you're saying, "Hey, look with me at what God is doing right now. Since he's at work there, you have every reason to keep working because you know your efforts will pay off." In its simplest form, encouragement is a way of saying, "I see glimpses now of the you that will exist forever in glory. I hope you see them too!"

> *Encouragement is much more than a pat on the back. It's inviting someone to become aware of the evidence in her life that shows God is at work.*

Carla's encouragement to her friend came in the form of a question: Do you realize that no one thinks about things like these? Sandy had been telling Carla about her morning. It was a cold day outside, and she had wanted to drive her kids to school. But they had not cooperated with her. They'd fooled around, taken forever to get ready, and found other things to do. Sandy had to let them walk their normal route to school so she could get to work on time. The kids understood and were not angry or upset with her, but she was unhappy about it.

She experienced a revelation as she drove down the road—the fact that what upset her had nothing to do with her kids. Instead, she was consumed by her own reputation, of not being able to think of herself as a good mom. She wanted to go to work believing she was considerate to her children, a nice mom who tried to make their lives easier. Then, when she couldn't drive them to school, she became unhappy—*not* because she had been a bad mom, but because she didn't get to think of herself as a nice person.

As she explored with the Lord how self-oriented her unhappiness was, she repented. Later she told Carla, who responded by saying, "I don't know of any other moms who even begin to think about their world this way!" That was encouraging to hear.

Struggling with sin that morning was ugly and lonely. Sandy faced the realization that she wasn't at all what she wanted to be. "Nice moms" don't use their children to bolster their own sense of self-worth. She needed to be cheered on in her pursuit of becoming more like Jesus. And Carla helped with her simple encouraging observation.

Healthy Relationships Will Communicate Forever

Sadly much of our present teaching, rebuking, and encouraging is set within the context of sin and suffering. One day that won't be true. Communication was not first introduced as an antidote to evil, as though it were merely a tool of sanctification. It made its appearance into the universe before sin stepped onstage, and it will still have a starring role in all our relationships long after evil has walked off. One day there will be no more darkness, but there will still be conversations.

Until that time, conversation is a primary tool that God uses to love us. He spoke when humans first abandoned him. He continued speaking when they wanted nothing to do with him. Thankfully, instead of growing silent, he became more vocal over time, until in these last days he has spoken to us by his Son (Hebrews 1:2). Having heard Jesus for ourselves, we now speak up and nurture each other by echoing what we've heard from the Word who became flesh.

On Your Own

1. Meditate on the wonder that it is for you to be a separate and distinct individual, yet vitally connected through your ability to communicate. When was the last time you thanked God for being able to connect with him and others?

2. What keeps you from speaking well to others? How does God's patient, persistent, never-ending conversation with you give you hope?

3. In which type of speaking are you strongest—teaching, rebuking, or encouraging? Which one do you need to develop? Who around you needs to hear "the very words of God" from you?

4. When there's no more sin and suffering, what are you going to talk to God about? If these elements of darkness shape no part of its content, how long a conversation can you hold with him now? Take a moment and try. How must that part of your future affect your present conversations with other people in his family?

CHAPTER 9

Serving Love: Helping Each Other

We're building a context for relationships that says "I am for you." Another aspect of that kind of love is serving others by offering physical help that matches the loving words you have spoken. This chapter explores serving love.

Serving love affects your relationships in two ways. First, when I serve you, I remind myself that I am not in this friendship for what I can get out of it as much as for how I can benefit you. Second, when you know you are clearly the beneficiary of my service, you gain greater confidence that you are special to me.

At least, those are the messages you and I *should* receive when I serve you. All too often, however, a whole range of mixed motives intrude, leaving me angling to get more than I give. When that happens, I'm actually chipping away at the relationship instead of building it.

Jesus never serves you to get something from you. His service is motivated initially by what you need, but it doesn't end there. He continues to serve you until he changes you—until you begin serving out of the same motives as his. Instead of duty or responsibility, you will find joy in meeting other people's needs without looking for something in return. Ironically, your happiness at being able to make someone else's life better will set the stage for people to move closer to you.

Jesus knew how necessary this aspect of love is. That's why he didn't stay in heaven, shouting down to us. He put on a body so that he could serve us in a way that we could see and feel, as well as hear.

> Now before the Feast of the Passover, when Jesus knew that his hour had come to depart out of this world to the Father, having loved his own who were in the world, he loved them to the end. During supper, when the devil had already put it into the heart of Judas Iscariot, Simon's son, to betray him, Jesus, knowing that the Father had given all things into his hands, and that he had come from God and was going back to God, rose from supper. He laid aside his outer garments, and taking a towel, tied it around his waist.
>
> Then he poured water into a basin and began to wash the disciples' feet and to wipe them with the towel that was wrapped around him. He came to Simon Peter, who said to him, "Lord, do you wash my feet?"
>
> Jesus answered him, "What I am doing you do not understand now, but afterward you will understand."
>
> Peter said to him, "You shall never wash my feet."
>
> Jesus answered him, "If I do not wash you, you have no share with me."
>
> Simon Peter said to him, "Lord, not my feet only but also my hands and my head!"
>
> Jesus said to him, "The one who has bathed does not need to wash, except for his feet, but is completely clean. And you are clean, but not every one of you." For he knew who was to betray him; that was why he said, "Not all of you are clean."

When he had washed their feet and put on his outer garments and resumed his place, he said to them, "Do you understand what I have done to you? You call me Teacher and Lord, and you are right, for so I am. If I then, your Lord and Teacher, have washed your feet, you also ought to wash one another's feet. For I have given you an example, that you also should do just as I have done to you. Truly, truly, I say to you, a servant is not greater than his master, nor is a messenger greater than the one who sent him. If you know these things, blessed are you if you do them. (John 13:1–17, *paragraph formatting added*)

We Would Rather Be Served Than Serve

When I was growing up I had what I thought was the worst job in my family. We had two large dogs that had a special talent: you could put large quantities of perfectly good food into one end and they would transform it into equally large quantities of stuff that was no longer food and certainly not good. My job was to remove the piles of non-good, non-food stuff from the backyard where they deposited them.

I hated that job. The idea alone was nauseating, and the stench was overpowering. I literally gagged almost every time. Honestly, changing my children's diapers years later was easier.

I remember a handful of mornings waking up to find that one of the dogs had been sick the night before—and smelling that non-good smell inside the house. I remember instantly developing a rare and curious ailment that made it impossible for me to detect odors— "Smell? What smell? No, I didn't notice anything."—because as you know, the first person to discover the source of the smell has the obligation to clean it up.

Did you catch what I was saying relationally? "I am here in this family not to give you all the best experience of life that I can, but to make my life as pleasant as possible." I didn't say it out loud, nor did I even consciously think it, but I did walk away from that moment having reinforced a destructive belief: relationships are all about me. At best, that belief poisoned me. I suspect it did more than that, however, as it came out in numerous other ways that undermined the foundation of relationships in my family. Frankly, it stank even worse than the odor in the house.

On the night Jesus was betrayed, he sat among his disciples at dinner, watching twelve guys do their best not to be the first to notice the needs of others.

The streets of Jerusalem were worse than my backyard. They were not modern, flat, asphalt affairs with gutters to collect excess water and refuse. At best, they were dry and dusty. At worst, trash and animal waste created an obstacle course that required you to walk through with care or take something home that you really didn't want. But your most careful navigating was useless when it rained. Then the "obstacles" melted, becoming evenly distributed so that everyone collected his fair share.[1]

Washing each other's feet in the ancient world was not simply a social nicety; it was a necessity. And it really was as nasty as it sounds. A job given to those furthest down on the social scale— not simply to your servant or child, but to the least of them.[2] Peers would consider it too demeaning to perform this task for each other, And so, that night at dinner no one seems to have been aware that there was even a problem: "Dirty feet? What dirty feet?"

It would have been impossible, however, not to notice. For dinner, people reclined around a low-lying table. It is probable that they lay on one side with their feet slightly behind them so that another person might lie alongside them. That means their feet would be close enough to each other that it would easily affect the mealtime. How could they be unaware?

Sadly, many people don't notice the needs others have or the opportunity to build their friendship by meeting those needs because they have trained themselves not to notice. This came home to my friend Rick as he was growing up. At a youth group event someone spilled a drink. Rick stood there staring at it, watching it spread, and only slowly realized, *I could do something to help clean this up.*

He was too late. While he had been standing there gazing at the mess, one of the girls from the group had already gotten up, found a mop, and brought it back. Rick saw the same thing she did, but he hadn't learned to consider what he needed do with what he saw. She saw a need that she could meet. He saw an accident that had nothing to do with him.

That's obscene. How can you be so unaware of others all around you with needs? If you can float through life without seeing the full picture of what's literally under your nose, then you have a strange kind of blindness: your eyes can see, but what they see doesn't affect what you do.

How can that be? How can children see, hear, and smell that their mom is getting dinner ready in the kitchen and yet not even think to ask how he or she can help? Or how can they clutter a playroom, then literally walk over, around, or on toys without noticing that they need to pick up the toys?

Grownups are also pretty gifted at not noticing things that need to be done. Do you have anyone in your life who doesn't mind leaving dirty dishes on the table or socks on the floor? Or who never thinks to lock up the house at night or turn the light off when they leave a room? Perhaps you have someone in your life who believes laundry washes and folds itself, refrigerators replenish their own shelves, checkbooks balance themselves, and cars change their own oil.

These kinds of examples get joked about at young married

couples' small groups. They seem so widespread that we tend to think of them as normal or their opposites as bizarre: Children who offer to help in the kitchen? What planet are you from?

As you watch the years go by, however, the jokes slowly turn from funny anecdotes to barbed sarcasm, to exasperated ranting, and finally to chilly silences. Why? Because when you live with someone who acts that way, you feel used. You feel taken for granted—like you're only an extension of what keeps their world working well. In other words, their lack of serving cuts at the heart of your friendship.

As upsetting as it is to be on the receiving end, if we're honest, this is true of all of us in some form or another. The reason we don't think about it too much is that we're more understanding of the way we strain relationships with our lack of serving than we are with the ways others affect us. This might be a good time for you to consider the relational messages you're sending people around you by the ways you make them serve you. Ask yourself if that's the way you want other people to experience you.

Sometimes people have taught themselves not to notice needs. At other times they do notice, but they are repulsed by the thought of serving. The diaper offends your nose. Driving your neighbor to the doctor's office is inconvenient. Helping with your son's school project or moving your friend will interrupt watching the playoff game. You're tired, you're busy, you already gave at the office. You see the need, but the cost is greater than you want to pay. There are many ways you can teach yourself to believe that someone else should take care of this need at this moment. I should be served instead.

The disciples could identify with that feeling. They weren't always good at serving. In fact, I can't think of any times recorded where they voluntarily stooped lower to help someone else. The times that stand out show just the opposite.

- They grew tired of serving (for example: when they preferred to send away the crowd who had been listening to Jesus all day, instead of feeding them [Mark 6:35–36]);
- They didn't want to be bothered by troublesome people (like when they tried to block little children from getting to the Lord [Luke 18:15]);
- They longed to be served (asking Jesus, immediately after he told them he's walking to his death, "Can we sit at the places of honor and privilege with you in glory?" [Mark 10:37, my paraphrase]).

As you flip through the Gospels, you can see that the disciples' willingness to serve does not stand out. What does grab your attention is Jesus' response. He made serving look attractive. Consider John 13 again.

Jesus Is among Us as One Who Serves

This is his last night on earth. He's about to endure suffering and humiliation that I cannot begin to describe. In his place, wouldn't you long for a little comfort? At least someone to wash your feet so you could enjoy your last meal without being grossed out by the guy next to you?

Would you remember the time when a prostitute showed real love by washing your feet with her tears, drying them with her hair, then dousing them with expensive perfume (Luke 7:36–50)? I can't imagine how tempting it would have been to look around the room at these "friends" and compare their love with that of the person others called "sinner."

Worse, wouldn't you hope that after these past several years they would have gotten it by now? They have been with you constantly, day in and day out, watching you give away every last drop of energy serving others. On this night, of all nights, shouldn't you have the gift of not having to look around the room at twelve grown men who are all too self-important to notice there's a problem?

How would you respond? Sigh deeply and say, "Would *somebody* please do *something* about the *feet?*" Or perhaps you would think for a moment about who hasn't been pulling his weight lately. "Um, Thomas. I think you've been slacking off a bit—how about you grab the basin?" After all, you know that your Father has given all things into your hands. You would be right to order someone to hop to it.

For that matter, what's a little dust and grime to the Creator of the universe? You could just snap your fingers, zap it all away, and get on with the meal. Surely you've more than earned a little ease and comfort on this night.

Maybe your thoughts would turn dark. You might find yourself ruminating over their thoughtlessness and self-absorption. Maybe you would turn their failings over and over in your mind until in frustration you lashed out at them. You could try to shame someone—all of them!—into scrambling to find a basin. And you would be able to justify your approach by telling yourself this was a really important lesson they needed to learn.

He was carrying such a burden that night. Surely he didn't need this one more thing. Yet, Jesus loved them to the very end (John 13:1). He really wasn't sick of them or how difficult they made his life. He loved them. And so, in his love, he served them. He got up from dinner, at which point the conversation must have faltered. He took off his clothes. Conversations stopped. He grabbed a towel—amid an uncomfortable silence. He filled a basin and started taking care of them. He did for them what they needed from him.

That's one of the keys to understanding this passage. His actions are so far removed from our experience that I suspect too often we turn them from honest service into a quaint ceremony.

I once participated in a foot-washing service that I remember chiefly for its awkwardness. My religious background didn't hold such services, but I had friends in college who came from a tradition that did. The idea was intriguing to me, partly for its novelty, but also as a way to express our desire to serve others. So our campus fellowship conducted one.

I found the night to be more uncomfortable than anything else. I recall a rhythm of praying (or looking like I was praying while I was frantically thinking, *What do I do next?*) and feeling pressure from within to do *something*, getting up to wash someone's feet, followed by more anxious prayer-thinking.

As I look back on that experience, I don't think the other leaders, staff, or members were at fault that night. What clunked for me was that foot-washing wasn't a true need for anyone with whom I rubbed shoulders in the twentieth century. Therefore, something that in the first century had been a service had morphed into mere ceremony by the time it got to my century. The symbolism was there, but it had lost traction because I failed to relate it to the real daily needs that existed around me. Now, if we had gone out and shaved or bathed the homeless, it might've been closer to the original act.

Jesus wasn't engaged in a ceremony. He wasn't putting on a show. He was a true servant who was simply doing what needed to be done. Servants don't perform so that people recognize them. They're not doing things that are unnecessary. Instead, they are consciously aware of the needs around them, and they do something about them.

Kyle and Morgan were meeting with my wife and me to talk about their marriage. Morgan was upbeat and mentioned how the past two weeks had been "really good." Primed as I was to hear a whole list of things Kyle was doing differently, I was somewhat surprised when Morgan talked only about how Kyle's attitude seemed better and that he had been unloading the dishwasher.

I realized there was something special beneath what she was

saying, and I didn't want them to miss the power that a "small thing" could have on the tone of their relationship. So I intention-ally asked a dumb question, "That's been so meaningful to you because it saves you hours and hours of time?"

> It's not always the size of our service that communicates love, but simply noticing what needs to be done and stepping in to do it.

"Well, not hours. It does help me," Morgan explained, "but even more it shows me he's thinking about me and that I'm important to him." That's what I thought she would say. It's not always the size of our service that communicates love, but simply noticing what needs to be done and stepping in to do it.

That's what Jesus did. He was among them as one who serves.

Jesus' Deeper Service to You

In serving his friends, Jesus intends to create a community of servants, of people who actively care for the needs of each other. In just a few minutes he's going to put his towel aside and resume being their Lord and Teacher. He's going to instruct them to follow his example in serving each other, just as he has served them. He sees this aspect of love as an ongoing, necessary part of their lives with each other. To underline its importance, he points to himself, reminding them that a servant is not greater than his master, nor is a messenger greater than the one who sent him (John 13:16).

It's a cool tagline. He used it regularly with them before (Matthew 10:24; Luke 6:40; 22:27). If they were not careful, however, they would misinterpret his example and set themselves up for failure. If earlier they had refused to serve, perhaps out of some mixture of stubbornness and pride, wouldn't they now be tempted to serve out of shame, embarrassment, or a sense of duty? Even worse, maybe now they'd serve so that others would recognize what great servants they were. Maybe if they served, Jesus would like them more!

That wouldn't be any better. Then they'd go through the motions of serving, but *still* not long to reach outside themselves to care for another. They'd have exchanged self-importance for self-righteousness as they looked better on the outside but remained self-focused on the inside. His ministry would have turned them into hypocritical legalists, which would have been just as disastrous to their friendships as their refusal to serve.

You face these same temptations in your relationships. Too often, Christians have leaned on these guilt-inducing tactics to compel people to care for each other. Have you ever heard something like "Jesus gave his life for you. Is it too much to ask that you would volunteer for nursery duty, help cut the grass, take a meal to a shut-in, or come to the special business meeting?" When duty, responsibility, and obligation become the motivating forces for serving, people respond with anything but joy and delight.

Sadly, having seen these strategies honored in our larger church settings, we feel free to use them with the people around us. We tell our kids, "After all I've done for you, it is high time for you to . . ." Or we think nothing of saying to a spouse, "I took out the trash, bathed the kids, cut the grass, trimmed the trees, fixed the backed-up sink, folded the laundry . . . now it's your turn." Is it any surprise that their response is grudging? Motivated by duty, they respond dutifully. They're being manipulated, and they know it.

While the I-have-done-for-you-now-you-do-for-me approach is most horrible in the bedroom, it never produces warm, openhearted connections anywhere. Our relationships will be crushed under duty and responsibility unless Jesus can do more than mere external cleansing. That's when you realize what Jesus does with water and dirty feet is a living parable. Through his actions he teaches them what they really need. He even acknowledges that they won't be able to understand what he's doing now, but later—after the cross—they would understand (John 13:7).

The dirty feet are not the biggest problem in the room—it's their dirty hearts. They are unclean in the place where cleanliness really counts. Their longings for power, prestige, and position stink far more than the dirt and filth of Jerusalem roadways. And it clings to their souls far more tightly than any earthly grime ever did to their bodies.

Even as he removes dirt and dust, he plans to remove far more. He's going to remove the scale and slime from their souls. He's going to give them a new heart that is pure and clean, just like his. It will be a heart that freely, gladly moves outside itself in order to care for the needs of others. Their new desire will move them quickly to do whatever others need without feeling guilted into it or superior after having done it. His actions at their feet are a pale reflection of what he'll do at the foot of the cross. He's going to make sure they are really clean. He's going to cleanse them of their sins.

Washing their feet is the outward expression of his heart's desire that they be clean through and through. And they must be clean if they're to have any friendship with him. If he does not wash them, cleanse them, and purify them, *then* they will not have any part of him.

And neither will you. You must willingly submit to his serving you in ways that you cannot serve yourself. If you refuse to allow him to clean you in the way he knows you need, you have no part in him. That's the whole point of being clean—so that you can be friends with Jesus. That's why Peter does such an abrupt about-face. Formerly, he considers it unthinkable that Jesus would wash his feet, but if the only way to a friendship with Jesus is to be washed by him, then Peter wants an entire bath!

Notice the path that serving takes. Jesus serves you, but you don't serve him in the same way. No one that night got up and then washed Jesus' feet. Not one of them would ever make him the least bit clean.

There isn't the barest hint in the room that night of a quid pro quo where he turns to the guys and says, "Okay, enough. I've done for you—now it's your turn to do for me!" Nor does he even suggest to them a way for them to pay him back. They're not equals in serving each other. Rather, he remains their Lord. Serving moves in one direction only: from him to you. But it doesn't end with you. It moves outwardly to the people around you.

He Cleanses You So You Can Serve

Serving gets passed along to others because when Jesus cleanses you, it's not so you can keep thinking everyone else should serve you. Being clean like Jesus means you now serve others with his attitude. Being clean allows you to realize that servants are highly valued in God's economy.

Do you skip over the genealogies in the Old Testament? You know, those long, boring lists of impossible-to-pronounce names? If so, you're in for a treat. Let yourself think carefully about the following list from 1 Chronicles (don't worry—I struggle with the names too):

> Over the king's treasuries was Azmaveth the son of Adiel; and over the treasuries in the country, in the cities, in the villages, and in the towers, was Jonathan the son of Uzziah; and over those who did the work of the field for tilling the soil was Ezri the son of Chelub; and over the vineyards was Shimei the Ramathite; and over the produce of the vineyards for the wine cellars was Zabdi the Shiphmite. Over the olive and sycamore trees in

the Shephelah was Baal-hanan the Gederite; and over the stores of oil was Joash. Over the herds that pastured in Sharon was Shitrai the Sharonite; over the herds in the valleys was Shaphat the son of Adlai. Over the camels was Obil the Ishmaelite; and over the donkeys was Jehdeiah the Meronothite. Over the flocks was Jaziz the Hagrite. All these were stewards of King David's property. (1 Chronicles 27:25–31)

That's a long list of people who are remembered thousands of years after they lived. Why? Because they were great warriors? No. It was because they took care of the king's fields, his vineyards, his produce, his herds, his camels, his flocks, and even his donkeys.

Isn't that great? God keeps track of who takes care of the donkeys.[3] One day in heaven you're going to be introduced to Jehdeiah the Meronothite, and you're going to exclaim, "Oh, Jehdeiah! You're the donkey keeper!" And you're going to know that because "servant" is not a curse word in God's vocabulary; it's a high calling. It's high enough to carve out space in his eternal Word so that you would remember into perpetuity those who serve.

Maybe that doesn't strike you as very spiritual. How many of us grew up longing to have the epitaph "He mucked out the donkey's stalls" engraved on our tombstones? But those physical activities are intensely spiritual because doing them is caring for people. That means there is tremendous *eternal* value in things like collecting the Communion cups, vacuuming the church carpet, changing diapers, and picking up the paper towel off the men's room floor that somehow always seems to miss the trash can.

Irma is a dear saint who faithfully sharpens the pencils in the pew racks weekly. That is spiritual service.[4] Now maybe you're thinking, *Oh, come on. Aren't you taking this a little too far? I mean, that's nice, but sharpening pencils is spiritual?* Absolutely.

Have you ever been touched by a song in church or by something someone shared and wanted to write it down? You forgot your pen that day so you reach for the pencil in front of you, but the point is broken. You tell yourself to remember the phrase, but before you leave the building, it's left your memory. Or during the announcements, someone will encourage visitors to write their name and needs on the card in front of them, but the card's been doodled on and the pencil has no eraser. The person gives up, and no one sends her a card or calls her or knows that she really could have used a meal this past week, a shoulder to cry on, or a listening ear. Now a sharpened pencil means a lot more than it did a moment ago.

The person who sharpens pencils and straightens cards is engaged in serious spiritual ministry, although you never think about him, and he never shows up on anyone's official ministry list. It's real ministry because it's connected to real people with real needs.

But Irma doesn't merely serve impersonally. Broadly serving her congregation is actually an extension of her love for the people immediately around her. After she finished with the pencils one week, I asked what else she planned to do that day. She's in her eighties and is a bundle of energy. She told me how she was buying shoes for an elderly shut-in . . . for the third time. Apparently the first two pairs of replacement shoes hadn't been the right size, so she was going back again. The lady in her nineties needed shoes because hers had been lost when Irma had taken her to the hospital.

Irma makes me feel tired. And whereas I would have grumbled and complained (to make sure everyone knew what a great servant I was), she was positive and upbeat. "We'll just keep buying them and taking them back until we find something that fits."

In God's kingdom there are no little acts of service, no trivial things

> In God's kingdom there are no little acts of service, no trivial things that don't mean much.

that don't mean much. In his kingdom the donkey-keepers, the pencil-sharpeners, and the shoe-buyers are memorialized. Just like the keeper of the donkeys, Irma's name is written down and remembered before God for all eternity. Hebrews 6:10 reminds us: "For God is not unjust so as to overlook your work and the love that you have shown for his name in serving the saints, as you still do." *He* will not forget the service she has rendered.

Learning to Serve

So having seen that God loves people by serving them and that he values the way we serve others, how do you learn to serve? There are two things to keep in mind.

First, stop assuming your friendships exist to cater to your desires or make your life easier. My lead pastor is constantly in and out of the church, meeting people all week. Since he packs his schedule with appointments, it's helpful if he has a place where he can quickly park at the church without wasting time. Staff have suggested for years that he get a sign designating the pastor's parking spot. He resisted until people made it harder and harder for him to find a place close to the building. So our property and grounds manager put one in for him.

Now we have a sign in front of a space that reads "Reserved Parking." It's set at windshield height so you can't miss it when you pull into the spot. And yet we've had more people park there now than before the sign was there. They all assume the spot is reserved for them. Isn't that amazing? They assume, *Oh, if I park here I'm not going to mess anything up. Whoever this is for obviously doesn't need it right now and won't until after I'm gone.* That thinking comes from the conviction that others exist to serve you.

If Jesus cleanses you, you can learn to make the opposite

assumption. You can learn to think, *No one's here now, but the person for whom this is reserved might come and need it. Therefore, on the off-chance that he or she will, I'm not going to use it. I will gladly make my life a little less easy in order to make someone else's better.* That's what it means to serve.

I came home early one night when I was in school so I could try to catch up on the things I'd let go around the house. They had been weighing heavily on my mind. One foot inside the door told me, however, that I had a choice: I could plow ahead with my agenda, but I was going to do so at Sally's expense.

She'd been home all day inside our basement apartment with our infant daughter. She was feeling physically and mentally exhausted. There was still tons of stuff to be done, but she had no more energy to do it. Worse, she felt like she hadn't had any time to just play with Cassie, and she was close to breaking down. By God's grace I told her, "I think you need a chance to go outside, see the sun, and just spend some fun time with Cass. Why don't you let me finish dinner and straighten up the kitchen?"

She really needed that help, and it set the tone for the rest of the evening. She came back in much happier, and we enjoyed being together. She knew that I cared about her and what she was going through. But in order to connect with her in that moment, I had to let my own plans go and believe she wasn't there simply to make my life easier.

That's the difference Jesus can make in your life. Do you remember the story I told at the beginning of this chapter about my unwillingness to clean up after our family pets? About how I believed relationships existed to serve me? The small changes in the way I relate to the people around me now encourage me because they show that being served by Jesus really does make the difference he promised it would.

Second, in order to serve, learn to look for where people need help. Did the snow just fill your seventy-three-year-old neighbor's driveway? Go help shovel it. Are the kids descending on your husband as soon as he comes in the door extra frazzled from work? Run interference for fifteen minutes while he recovers from the day. Is your single friend turning thirty and feeling lonely? Find out if anyone is organizing a special birthday party for her. Has your wife been making dinner for the past two weeks? Cook on the weekends or call her one morning to say, "I'll stop on the way home and pick something up." Is Mother's Day coming up and you know Dad just doesn't celebrate well? Ask him what you can do to help. Does the laundry need folding, the shelves need dusting, the car need vacuuming, the grass need cutting, the shower need cleaning?

You get the picture. Serving is not hard. Most of the time it simply takes a willingness to notice and a greater willingness to be involved. These are all small things, to be sure, but they communicate a big heart—a heart that wants to be involved with your friends for their benefit. A heart that shows you have tasted God's heart for you.

> *Serving is not hard. Most of the time it simply takes a willingness to notice and a greater willingness to be involved.*

When you do this, a funny thing will happen. You'll want even more people to taste that heart. So you'll look around and learn to go where other people don't want to go. You'll enter homes that are broken down or lives that are broken down. You'll get your hands dirty by cleaning the house of someone who can't. You'll watch someone's children so she can go to work, to counseling, to court, or to her support group. You'll take people a meal when they can't make it themselves and are too proud to ask.

You will throw away old patterns of waiting for people to come to you with their needs. Instead, you'll let yourself notice what needs to be done. Then you'll interrupt your dinner, your television time, your vacation, your lifestyle, your career goals, and your retirement plans, and you'll get up. You'll take off the outer-clothing identity you've worked so hard to have—of being a decent, hard-working, reliable person who deserves a break today—and you'll put on the clothes of a servant, someone who does the necessary but menial chores that no one else wants to do. And then, like your Lord did for you, you will go to the people around you and gladly give yourself to meet their needs.

On Your Own

1. Meditate on how Jesus has served you. Think both historically and from your present experience. How has he cleansed you? What other needs has he met for you in the past several days?

2. Do you like a God who serves you even if you can't repay him? What characterizes your response to him—stunned silence, belligerent rejection, grateful acceptance . . . ? Talk to him about your reaction to him.

3. What needs do you typically overlook? What service do you dislike? What keeps you from serving—a belief that you are not responsible or that someone else should be responsible, a feeling of repulsion, a fear of being vulnerable . . . ? Seek Christ's cleansing again, and ask him to renew your desire to help others.

4. Think about the needs of the people closest to you. How might you help them? Think outside the narrow, normal ways that Americans feel comfortable. Now go beyond. What needs does your church have? Your community? Who might serve with you?

CHAPTER 10

Providing Love: Meeting Physical Needs

Closely related to serving love is providing love. Providing love supplies someone else's physical needs. Many times these two aspects of love are intertwined. Serving love and providing love are difficult to distinguish when you take a friend out to lunch whose paycheck is a little thin this month. The difference is that while the previous chapter focused on the necessary aspect of *doing* to meet someone's need, this chapter looks more closely at *giving* to the people around you.

Once again, this is an important, ongoing part of the way God loves you. He has promised to feed you, clothe you, and take care of all of your needs (see Genesis 1:29; 9:3; Matthew 6:25–34). He proactively notices what you need to live on earth and moves to provide those things, giving you a daily reminder of how important and special you are to him.

Knowing he will provide all you need frees you, in turn, to shift the focus in your relationships from yourself to others. You will enjoy moving from an inward focus that asks how can knowing others benefit me to an outward, generous impulse that longs to know what others need.

God's Miraculous Provisions Operate within a Mundane World

If you had all the power God has at his disposal, it would be so easy to meet your friends' needs, wouldn't it? Jesus makes a meal for five thousand people out of five loaves and two fish. How would you like that ability at Thanksgiving when you're running late in putting the meal together? He cures sicknesses, takes away fevers, returns sight to blind eyes, and removes paralysis and even leprosy. Wouldn't that be a great skill when you or your children are up half the night with an uncontrollable cough that medicine doesn't seem to touch?

Recall what he does when Peter is asked about whether or not his master pays the temple tax:

> When they came to Capernaum, the collectors of the two-drachma tax went up to Peter and said, "Does your teacher not pay the tax?" He said, "Yes." And when he came into the house, Jesus spoke to him first, saying, "What do you think, Simon? From whom do kings of the earth take toll or tax? From their sons or from others?" And when he said, "From others," Jesus said to him, "Then the sons are free. However, not to give offense to them, go to the sea and cast a hook and take the first fish that comes up, and when you open its mouth you will find a shekel. Take that and give it to them for me and for yourself." (Matthew 17:24–27)

How would you like to have that ability come April 15 when your taxes are due? I've seen love like that lavished on me. Finding a fifty-dollar bill on the ground as an impoverished student or a pack-age of subway tokens as an even more impoverished high school teacher were instances to me of God's special love. I'm sure you have stories of his miraculous provision as well.

The widow of 2 Kings 4:1–7, whose sons were about to be taken as slaves in order to pay her debts, received provision. Elisha had her borrow as many empty jars as she could and start filling them from her oil jar. Miraculously, she was able to fill all the other jars, giving her enough oil to sell so that she could pay her debts and live off the rest—and keep her sons.

Miraculous, yes. But stop and think a moment because this isn't as supernatural as it could be. Totally miraculous would be simply a pile of money appearing in her home—or better yet, have it ap-pear in the homes of the people she owed, along with a little note: "From God for the widow—leave her alone." Miraculous oil, yes. But there was much human effort involved in collecting the jars and selling the oil. If you had the ability to simply wave a wand and deal with people's needs, would you mix commonplace means in as well? Wouldn't you continue to dot the sidewalks with fifty-dollar bills that your friends could pick up as needed?

If you think about it a little longer, you see that Jesus does the same thing his Father does. Why should Peter catch the fish? Why not just put the money in his hand? Even more astonishing to me—since I would be tempted to use miracles all the time if I had the power—are the times when he doesn't seem to use any supernatural means at all. Look at how he cooks breakfast for his followers after he's risen from the dead, with not even a hint of anything out of the ordinary.

When they got out on land, they saw a charcoal fire in place, with fish laid out on it, and bread. Jesus said to them, "Bring some of the fish that you have just caught." So Simon Peter went aboard and hauled the net ashore, full of large fish, 153 of them. And although there were so many, the net was not torn. Jesus said to them, "Come and have breakfast." Now none of the disciples dared ask him, "Who are you?" They knew it was the Lord. Jesus came and took the bread and gave it to them, and so with the fish. This was now the third time that Jesus was revealed to the disciples after he was raised from the dead. (John 21:9–14)

How simple it would have been to instantly make them feel full, or simply to multiply the fish that he already had, or even to "zap" the fish from the nets over to the coals. He doesn't do that. He works through physical means: "Go, bring some more fish." And he does so without detracting from his spirituality.

As amazed as I am at the miracles Jesus does, I am learning to be more amazed at how *few* he does compared to how many he could do. When God loves you by providing for your needs, he often does so from within the parameters of a very physical world. The strength and abilities he's given me have made it possible for me to earn many times the amount of money I've found lying around on city streets. Jesus is incredibly physical as he operates inside of the normal parameters that God set for this planet. He cares for his friends' physical needs, yet gladly works through normal means to do so.

This aspect of love may be harder for our modern, Westernized minds to grasp. We tend to have expectations of our "natural world" that remove a sense of the miraculous from daily life. For instance, we come to expect food in the grocery store. If pressed, we would explain its presence not as evidence of the extraordinary work of God, but as the natural consequences of a process that starts with someone correctly tending crops and livestock. Such an explanation, however, misses the active work of God in caring for you.

My friend returned from Kenya and talked about how one of his hostesses, who enjoyed a modern lifestyle in many ways, froze him with a pointed look before eating. "We *must* thank God for this food that we're about to receive," she said. Her prayer was no mere show or habit, but a heartfelt appreciation for God's provision, knowing that he didn't owe it to them and that it could easily be otherwise. She knew she was being loved by her heavenly Father. There was a sense of God's extraordinary care and presence at that meal that I and many of my friends lack.

For us, God's daily provision seems far from miraculous. It recedes into the background of our consciousness, becoming a taken-for-granted expectation of the world in which we live. That false expectation affects our relationship with God in two ways. It keeps us from seeing his present miracles in caring for us, and it builds in us the belief that God's special love for his people will be seen in mysterious, unexplainable ways that operate outside our normal experiences.

The Real Miracle Is People Caring for Each Other

It should come as no surprise to you by now that the way God operates with you is the same way he looks for you to love those around you. He doesn't expect you to see someone else's need and hope that somehow it magically gets met. You're supposed to roll up your sleeves and pitch in to see what role you might have in meeting it. That's what you see take place in the early church. They had exactly the same concern to meet each other's physical needs as Jesus did when he was on earth.

And all who believed were together and had all things in common. And they were selling their possessions and belongings and distributing the proceeds to all, as any had need.

Now the full number of those who believed were of one heart and soul, and no one said that any of the things that belonged to him was his own, but they had everything in common. And with great power the apostles were giving their testimony to the resurrection of the Lord Jesus, and great grace was upon them all. There was not a needy person among them, for as many as were owners of lands or houses sold them and brought the proceeds of what was sold and laid it at the apostles' feet, and it was distributed to each as any had need. (Acts 2:44–45; 4:32–35)

Amazing! These people didn't think any of their possessions were their own, but they felt they were to be used for the good of whoever needed them. They even cared for people they weren't blood related to because they had experienced a deeper, more radical kinship. Yes, they were saved as individuals, but they were saved into a family. Therefore, it only made sense to them to care for each other. Sounds pretty wonderful, and pretty convicting.

And just as amazing, they did it through normal, nonmiraculous means. If supernatural means of providing for others were ever to be normative for the way God intends to meet our needs, then this is the time when you'd expect to see it. These are the glory days of the church when the Holy Spirit chose to act in stunningly supernatural ways on a daily basis. These are the days of miracles and flashy signs done by the apostles: tongues of flame, healed paralytics, jail cells opened—even healings when people were touched by someone's shadow or handkerchief. It was a time full of miracles.

Not only that, but they're worshipping the same miraculous Jesus who recently fed a multitude in a desolate place. It was an extraordinary act that echoed how his Father made manna appear in the wilderness for forty years to provide for more than two million people. This God could easily have taken care of the early church's physical needs through similar supernatural means. But he didn't. Instead, his people took the burden of each other's needs and reached out to care for them.

That should be true of how you love the people around you as well. A mark that shows we have been brought into God's family is that we care about the physical welfare of the rest of the family. Now, lest you think this is just a Jewish way of handling needs, consider the characteristics of the Gentile Christians that show they are full-fledged members of God's family. First, they received the Holy Spirit, like their Jewish brothers and sisters had (Acts 10:44–46). Later, you see them studying and learning about their God, like their Jewish brothers and sisters had earlier (11:25–26). And then they gave their resources to help others.

> *A mark that shows we have been brought into God's family is that we care about the physical welfare of the rest of the family.*

> Now in these days prophets came down from Jerusalem to Antioch. And one of them named Agabus stood up and foretold by the Spirit that there would be a great famine over all the world (this took place in the days of Claudius). So the disciples determined, everyone according to his ability, to send relief to the brothers living in Judea. And they did so, sending it to the elders by the hand of Barnabas and Saul. (Acts 11:27–30)

Just like their Jewish brothers and sisters, they reduced their lifestyle by taking from their own pockets to help people they had never met. They responded to God's heart for those in need and showed that they loved like he loves. You can see the importance they place on those relationships by what it cost them to keep them. Little shows what you really believe like what you spend your resources on—your money, time, and expertise. It's when you give of your treasures to the people around you—or when you don't—that you show how much you value them.

> What good is it, my brothers, if someone says he has faith but does not have works? Can that faith save him? If a brother or sister is poorly clothed and lacking in daily food, and one of you says to them, "Go in peace, be warmed and filled," without giving them the things needed for the body, what good is that? So also faith by itself, if it does not have works, is dead. (James 2:14–17)

The book of Acts shows that people really believed God had connected them relationally into one body. Therefore, they acted accordingly, knowing that they were responsible for each other's welfare. Their actions resulted in the elimination of needs among them. This was no socialist movement devoid of the gospel. This was an opportunity to share the love of Christ in a real, visible, tangible way that pointed beyond the activity itself to the God whose heart is evidenced through his care.

This starts by first taking notice of the needs of those around you. Before you can take on the needs of people you don't know, you need to care for those you do. Start with your smallest circle of relationships. When was the last time you intentionally sat down and made a list of the needs your family has? Your friends? Maybe you want to include your neighbors as well. Don't start by thinking of all the reasons why there isn't anything you can do or by being overwhelmed by what you see. Begin simply training yourself to notice what other people need.

> Before you can take on the needs of people you don't know, you need to care for those you do. Start with your smallest circle of relationships.

Practicing Generosity

Making sure that there are no needy persons among us is a commitment to proactively look for what others need. Obviously, providing has a reactionary element to it. When your spouse or roommate tells you "The microwave is broken," you try to get it fixed. Providing love, however, goes beyond simply responding to what others tell you by actively looking for what people need.

Start with the people nearest you. The adage "Charity begins at home" follows Paul's admonition that we first take care of the needs of our families (1 Timothy 5:8). Do you think about the kids' shoes before they tell you their feet hurt? Is your spouse's car in good, safe, well-maintained condition? Does the condition of your parents' home concern you? Do you need to offer help in some way?

Are there conditions you make others who live with you put up with? When Matt, who is not a handyman, spent hours learning to scrape wallpaper, spackle and paint, then redo the caulking and grout in the bathroom, it meant the world to his wife. It was a very physical, tangible way he loved her, and she knew it.

Do you experience joy in providing for others? In bringing home a paycheck so that they can have food, clothes, a home, and some things they like? Are you happy to do so even when no one thanks you or seems to notice? Are there things you need to change now in your occupation so that you'll be able to better take care of future needs? Yes, you can over-care about money, but it is just as easy to not care enough. Have you thought about taking out an insurance policy that will help provide for the people who depend on you if you're no longer around?

Providing love also branches out and considers how your friends might need a little help. Maybe you decide to drop off a bag of groceries to someone who is out of work or take them on a shopping trip. Maybe you have friends who can't afford to go on a marriage retreat or take their family on vacation, but you know they really could use the time. So you work to make that happen. Better yet, you join with others to send them. I know of several people who pooled their resources to help a friend with an unexpected medical bill she couldn't pay. Loving others well sometimes means shouldering bills together.

Notice that we're moving beyond simple one-on-one giving here. God always intended that providing love would happen within a larger network of relationships. That's what happened with the manna in the wilderness. They shared the food they picked up off the ground so that "whoever gathered much had nothing left over, and whoever gathered little had no lack. Each of them gathered as much as he could eat" (Exodus 16:18). Paul revives that phrase when he wants to help the Corinthians understand that genuine concern for the corporate needs of others is what lies at the heart of their own giving impulse (2 Corinthians 8:15).

Without a community commitment to provide for each other's needs, the smaller examples will go unsupported for lack of access to the broader resources God intended. It is that larger commitment that sets the pace for the more individual expressions.

I know of a young single mother who received anonymous checks at Christmas from church members so she could buy presents for her children. It's hard not to be able to celebrate when everyone else is. That was one way her church loved her and her family.

On a more formal scale, I've known of churches where the staff gives out gift cards in order to spread the wealth around. These are small ways to say "We love you and we want to bless you. We are thinking of you."

A deacon once confided to me, "You can't ask people if they need anything because they'll tell you 'I'm fine.' So you just have to go to them. I give gift cards to the local convenience store. That way they can get milk, bread, gas, whatever they need. Those don't seem to get turned down!"

Sometimes help has to be bigger—taking care of a utility bill, passing along a used vehicle, or helping set someone up in an apartment. There are times when people need help financially because they mismanage their money, and there are also many times they struggle, not because their expenses are too great, but because their income is not great enough. Either way, it's in those times that the quality of our one-anothering is seen in how we open our wallets to each other.

Can you imagine donating your used car to a church so that they can give it to someone who either doesn't have one or whose vehicle is in bad shape? How about hiring a contractor who is out of work? You planned to get to that job next year, but his need is now and you have the funds, so why not?

Where else can you love the way God does by deliberately not having all you could so that someone else will benefit (2 Corinthians 8:9)? I was amazed the day I saw the church caring for people's needs when two ladies handed me a check for the counseling center. They had decided to forgo giving each other a Christmas present and donate the money so that we could serve needy people who couldn't afford their own counseling. Having no needs among you is a glorious thing that proclaims to the universe the meaning of real love.

This is not just for people with lots of means. This is for anyone who takes the time to think about the needs of others. When my middle son, Timmy, was six years old, he sidled up to me just as Sally and I were about to head out for a date, and he tried to slip me some money. In a conspiratorial whisper he said, "Here's a quarter so you can buy Mom a pretzel."

That's love. He's not thinking about what I can do for him in that moment. Nor is he focused on what he doesn't have. He's thinking about what might benefit someone else, and he's not allowing his own lack to interfere with what he might give. That's something both you and I can learn to do.

How Providing Love Affects People

When you meet people's needs, you affect them in ways that words alone cannot. First, your friend knows she is loved and cared for.

Before I became part of our church staff, the lead pastor asked me when I had last taken my wife away for a night. Between the realities of a ministry income and three small children, it had been a really long time. I babbled a bit incoherently as I cast my mind back, unsuccessfully trying to recall the last time. He interrupted my disjointed answer by sliding a brochure over to me for a bed and breakfast and said, "Here's a place we like to send people so they can be refreshed. Do you want to pick out a night so that we can send you and Sally?"

I went home and told Sal, and she cried. We hadn't experienced care like that too often. I went back and told him which day we were thinking and he said, "Great, do you want one night or two?" And this wasn't a dumpy place either. It had really posh rooms, including whirlpool, gas fireplace, a shower that was larger than my entire bathroom at home, and a gourmet breakfast. This was all before we even started attending the church!

Do you have any idea what that meant to us? It is amazing to have someone reach out to you and do something that is simply for your benefit without looking for anything in return. It touches you deeply. You cry. You know you are loved and cherished. Not for anything you add, but simply because you exist. You are invited to remember that being made in God's image is reason enough to be valued.

The experience became even more helpful as it reminded me that I needed to reintroduce into our marriage times away with Sally. I had been careful early in our marriage to make special "us" dates and weekends, but had gotten away from doing so. That omission was detrimental. Someone else caring for our relationship helped me take more responsibility for us as a couple.

A second effect of caring for each other's needs is that doing so creates breathing space. The burdens and difficulties of life can be crushing at times. It feels literally like the walls are closing in and there's little you can do about it. In those moments, you need practical, outside help.

One evening I was opening birthday cards when out fell a check along with a note that said, "For your new reading chair." That took me by surprise as I didn't know anything about a reading chair, but I found the same thing in several of the envelopes. Our children were getting older and staying up later, and Sally realized how much I struggle to find a quiet place at night to decompress from the day. So she decided to do something about it.

When family had called to ask what I'd like for my birthday, she'd suggested contributions toward a chair for the office so I could have a place to recover from one day and set up the next. That may seem like a small thing, but it meant a great deal to me to know that she was trying to lighten the weight I felt. Sally and I have learned to think in those ways in part from being in a church that puts a premium on caring for each other's physical needs.

Kayla sat in the balcony at church and raised her hand during the announcements to get the pastor's attention. When he didn't seem to notice, she began waving her arm in broad sweeps that had to be acknowledged. Realizing she was not about to be ignored, he called up to her, "Good morning, Kayla!"

"Pastor, can I share something?"

"Sure, Kayla, go ahead."

"My husband left me and my son a year ago and we had to move out of our house into an apartment. I lost my job a few months back and so they kicked us out two weeks ago. We'd been sleeping at friends' homes and in my car for the past several days. Then this church found us a place to stay and we are so happy."

Kayla went on, trying to help several hundred people that morning understand what her one-room apartment meant to her. She described it as an incredible gift that she and her son were so thankful for—a place where they could safely be together and regroup as they tried to get back on their feet. For them, it halted a downward spiral and gave her hope that she could rebuild her life again. When someone steps into your world to relieve some of the pressure, it gives you a new lease on life.

Byron knew what that kind of pressure was like. "Hi," he said to the staff worker in charge of food distribution that night at church. "I'm the Johnsons' neighbor. I've been out of work for six months now." Byron, along with eighty other people who had little to nothing left to feed their families, gratefully filled boxes and bags with food that would keep them going for several days.

You could see and feel their relief. "I'm eating better during a recession!" one lady said as she picked up specialty food items donated by a local store. Another person there that night later e-mailed a detailed account of the ways God was providing for his family through the kindness of others.

Life was still tough for them, but now it was a little less overwhelming. A bit of light could shine through. They were less anxious because at least they knew where tomorrow's meal was. The walls were not closing in quite as quickly or as tightly as they had been earlier because they knew that others were in the struggle with them, caring for them.

Third, caring for each other's needs often provides the catalyst that someone needs to take charge of his own life again. A couple we barely knew visited one night and asked what we planned to do with our kitchen floor. (For the previous two years we'd been living on the subfloor, the rough foundation boards that span the joists.) I told them how my hope was to connect the kitchen with the dining room by laying hardwood flooring across both. The husband nodded thoughtfully, then said, "We can do this."

It turned out he installed floors for a living and knew exactly what to do. The floor came out beautifully. But that wasn't all. He came back a year later and helped put hardwood on our second floor as well.[1] In doing that, he kicked into gear a process that had been languishing.

We'd lived in the house for six years. Although I'd done much remodeling, there was still much to do, and, frankly, I was more than a little tired. His offer motivated me to return to projects that I'd let slide so that the second floor took a giant leap toward being finished. I would not have gotten there without people helping me move forward.

A fourth effect of others caring for my needs has been to help me see things in Scripture that I'd never seen before. Not too long ago I reread Genesis 47. In that passage Joseph introduces his father and brothers to Pharaoh. Pharaoh then responds.

> "Your father and your brothers have come to you. The land of Egypt is before you. Settle your father and your brothers in the best of the land. Let them settle in the land of Goshen, and if you know any able men among them, put them in charge of my livestock." (Genesis 47:5–6)

Now, you have to read this passage the way Jesus taught his disciples—that everything in the Scripture has something to do with helping you see him more clearly.[2] Think about the picture Genesis 47 presents. The ultimate ruler of the land is saying to his second in command, "All of your relatives are to get the absolute best I can give them."

Do you see your heavenly Father—the ultimate ruler of the universe—in this picture? Can you hear him as he speaks to the second most important person in the universe, his Son, and says to him, "Bring to me all those who are related to you, your brothers and sisters, and give them the best we have"? That narrative provides hints of the rich colors and textures behind what Paul says more directly in Romans:

> What then shall we say to these things? If God is for us, who can be against us? He who did not spare his own Son but gave him up for us all, how will he not also with him graciously give us all things? (Romans 8:31–32)

If you've got Jesus, you already have the best there is. And yet God would *graciously give* you even more. More than his Son? Can you even imagine what that means? It is amazing to ponder God's indescribable generosity.

For far too long I had read those passages without any insight into them. I didn't get excited about knowing this God because I missed seeing his character and his actions. I only began to understand him after I experienced the way my brothers and sisters here on earth cared for me in physical ways. Their generosity helped me see my God more clearly than I had before, because their care mirrored his heart.

On Your Own

1. On the scale of 1 to 10, how do you view God's concern for your physical well-being (1 = extreme penny-pinching miser;

10 = generous beyond imagining)? How have your experiences of Christian community contributed to your beliefs about God's desire to care for all your needs?

2. What would the church lose if God met physical needs in purely miraculous ways?

3. What does your concern for others' physical needs say about your experience of the gospel? Is it easier for you to ask for help or offer help? Where is Jesus inviting you to grow as part of a community that works toward having no needy persons among them?

4. Who around you has needs that Jesus longs to meet through your involvement? Have you noticed the needs before? If not, what has kept you from doing so? If you have noticed them but not done anything about them, what has held you back?

PART III

LOVE THAT ENJOYS HEAVEN ON EARTH

In heaven, sin and suffering will no longer have a role in how we relate to each other. But love will. In the future, pure, wholesome, healthy, engaging, delightful, enjoyable relationships will be the norm.

However, we don't have to wait until heaven to experience those aspects of love. Many of them are available now. That's because one of the glories of love is that it's a present experience of things that will unfold even more fully later.

You have not joined the kingdom of a slave-master. The church is no socialist experiment gone awry so that life is now lived in varying shades of grime and gray. Instead, you are part of a kingdom where joy is commanded because joy is at the very heart of your God and at the heart of your relationship with him. He is a happy God whose people develop joyful, peaceful relationships with each other as they become like him.

That kind of love cannot be contained. The more you develop your ability to love, the wider the circles of people who will experience it from you. By its very nature, love grows to encompass anyone who crosses your path, not only those you know well.

In Part III we will look at ways that loving well allows us to enjoy each other now as hints and shadows of what we'll experience for eternity. This is the kind of love that says "Let's enjoy the goodness of our relationship." In keeping with the expanding character of love, we will look beyond our more immediate relationships to encompass the broader communities we're part of.

Chapters in Part III:

11. Welcoming Love: Greeting Each Other

12. Humble Love: Submitting to Each Other

13. Celebrating Love: Rejoicing with Each Other

14. Peaceful Love: Living Harmoniously with Each Other

15. Hospitable Love: Showing Kindness without Grumbling

CHAPTER 11

Welcoming Love: Greeting Each Other

One important way we communicate how much we enjoy being with someone is by the way we greet each other. From the first moments of any interaction, you know whether or not you're wanted. Her words, attitude, facial expression, and body position clearly convey whether she's glad to be with you or wishes one of you was someplace else.

God understands how important an ongoing, openhearted embrace is to the rest of the relationship, which is why he greets people so well. He calls you by name, is glad to be with you, and longs to embrace you when you stray. Those elements let you know you are wanted and celebrate the relationship that exists between you.

They are just as important for you to bring to your human friendships as well.

This chapter looks at welcoming love, the kind of love that works to create an inviting atmosphere from the first moment you interact with people you already know.

God Greets People

On nine separate occasions in the New Testament we are told to greet people. That doesn't include the greater number of times we learn from the examples of others who send their greetings. Paul makes the point abundantly clear in Romans 16 as he tells the Roman Christians to greet thirty-three different people or groups of people who are on his heart.

A lot of space is taken up in Holy Scripture with a fairly ordinary activity that you might think is simply an outdated cultural way of closing a letter. When was the last time you invested significant time to refuel your spiritual energies by meditating on one of these greetings passages? Maybe you find them more irritating than anything else and so you tend to skip them. At first glance, they don't seem worthy of rising to the level of things you would make sure to include in a holy book. Surprisingly, however, the Bible is often concerned with the mundane things of life.[1]

You would expect a book that purports to guide you in reconnecting with God to have lots of "spiritual" information, wouldn't you? I'd expect it to be chock-full of instructions on how to have a devotional time, the nuts-and-bolts of meditating, and detailed descriptions of spiritual beings and places. To my surprise, it has almost none of those. Instead it spends a lot of time on what to eat, with whom you can have sex, and how to pay your taxes. It's concerned for how you talk, how you work, and how you care for others who are less privileged.

The Bible is not a magical book of formulas and instructions for having otherworldly mystical experiences. God is concerned for real, raw, physical life. So he makes sure you understand how vitally important it is . . . to greet each other. Keep digging and you learn that greeting others is an important spiritual activity because it reflects how our God interacts with his people.

"Okay," I can hear you say, "but so what? How can such a mundane activity have any significant effect on my relationships?" Consider this contrast: a man who is a husband and father who knows he's wanted by the way his family greets him at night when he comes home, compared to a man who is either hardly acknowledged when he walks in the door or who is instantly barraged with a list of wants and demands. All other things being equal, which man do you think might be more likely to stray into an affair with his newly divorced colleague at the office?

While greeting someone well is not a guarantee that you'll keep his loyalty, it sure gives him more of a reason to resist temptation and come home than the other guy has. The way he's greeted tells him how he is valued. The same is true of your relationship with God. You know you are valued by the way he takes the initiative to greet you, despite the fact that it seems like a relatively small thing.

That is not what I expect of someone who is infinitely above me in every way. We intuitively understand that important people do not introduce themselves. After all, what human dignitary doesn't have someone announce him or her? You don't expect a judge, ambassador, or head of state to introduce him or herself. To do so would diminish his importance in the eyes of those around him. Someone else does that for them.

The bailiff calls out, "All rise, the honorable Judge Jenkins presiding." Or a musical fanfare sets the stage for a dignitary's entrance. Then an announcement is made of the person's presence. Consider the State of the Union Address. Once the House, Senate, and special guests are seated, the Sergeant of Arms for the House of Representatives announces, "Mister/Madam Speaker, the President of the United States." It is only *then* that the president actually begins greeting people personally and the nation as a whole.

It would dishonor the president personally and the office in general *not* to introduce him and to require him to introduce himself.

In the normal course of affairs, he cannot afford to take the initiative to greet someone personally. So he waits to be introduced.

Not God.

This is the one person in the universe who could rightfully consider himself the center of everyone's attention, yet he doesn't act like it. Instead of presenters and fanfare that would distance him from his creatures, he gets personally involved. Although high and holy, he doesn't put space between himself and his creatures. Instead, he forges connections that begin with simple contact. He greets people. He draws you into a deeper relationship with himself by welcoming you. As I study how he greets people, I learn from him.

He Greets People by Name

Abraham was a wandering nomad far from home. Hagar was a woman known only by her occupational relationship to her mistress. Moses was an outlawed outcast in the wilderness. At a time in their lives when practically no one knew them or acknowledged them, God met each of these people and greeted them by name (Genesis 15:1; 16:8; Exodus 3:4). He let them know that, though they were radically unknown by those around them, *he* knew who they were. His form of greeting let them know he hadn't overlooked them. By dealing with them personally, he let them know how special they were to him.

Do you realize he knows your name too? Even if you are not important in other people's eyes, you are incredibly special and unique to him. Revelation 2:17 tells us that God will give a new name to those who overcome, a name unknown except to the one who receives it. You will have your own name, shared by nobody else. In heaven, God will call out your name and no one else will turn their head or accidentally answer for you.

Having grown up with the name Bill Smith I can tell you how special that is. When I sat in a class with Otis Taylor, I broke the eleventh commandment about not coveting thy neighbor's name. Over the course of my life I have never met another Otis Taylor. But Bill Smith? Do you have any idea how many times I've signed into a hotel only to have the desk clerk wink at me and say, "Oh, right. Nice to have you with us Mr. *Smith*." And each one thinks it's the first time I've ever heard the joke.

There is a sign posted in my neighborhood that advertises a medical practice for a Dr. William P. Smith. Not only does this guy have my name, but my title and even my middle initial.

Heaven will be different. There will be no confusion when God calls out my name; no one else's head will turn. In Revelation we see him giving out unique names because he relates to us as distinct individuals from the first time he starts the conversation. When he greets people he's thinking of the one-and-only, special individual in front of him, whom he knows by name. He knows your name too—even if no one else thinks you're special.

There's a world of difference, however, between knowing someone's name and liking that person. In fact, you could probably think right now of several people whose names you wouldn't say with a smile. So you don't simply want to know that God singles you out. You also want to know what his attitude is when he calls your name.

He Is Excited to See You

The Song of Solomon has long been understood to operate at both a human and a divine level. In this passionate—at times erotic— dialogue between two lovers, you learn about the goodness and excitement of committed, romantic relationships between married people. But, just as Paul's discourse between husbands and wives in Ephesians 5 is intended to help you understand Christ and his bride, so the Song of Solomon is intended to help you to look beyond human interactions to glimpse the relationship between God and his people. He takes the role of the Lover, while his people are the Beloved.[2]

And as his people's Lover, he is absolutely enthralled. He marvels over their beauty, longs to hear their voice, and realizes that he no longer owns his own heart (see Song of Solomon 4:1–15; 6:4–9; 7:1–9; 8:13; and 4:9–10, respectively). He is smitten. Absolutely head over heels in love.

And his bride knows it. She sees him "leaping over the mountains, bounding over the hills" just to see her (Song of Solomon 2:8). She knows he can't wait until they're together again. When they reunite, he welcomes her with his whole heart and his attitude. This is a woman who knows she is wanted because he lets her know it with everything he has. He's excited. He's enthusiastic. He's goofy-in-love!

Does it sound odd to talk about God like that? Does it offend you? Is it a little too undignified? He started it. He gave you a picture of a meeting that invites you to see his unbridled enthusiasm. He comes running to you and declares that he acts this way toward you because it's the way he feels about you. His manner of greeting matches his words. He wants to be with you, and he wants you to be with him.

> You don't need any specialized training. All you need to do is step outside of yourself long enough to smile at someone and make the effort to let him know how you feel about seeing him.

I wish you could meet my pastor right now. I love to hear his booming "*Good* morning!" roll out of the office and down the hall when he arrives in the morning. He has a quick, infectious smile that you just have to return. When he gives you a bear hug and announces to everyone present, "I've decided—we like Chris! Amen," you know you're loved and wanted. His feelings come out in his welcome. There is no doubt that he's glad you're there because the way he greets you makes sure you know it. Notice that he does nothing the rest of us cannot do. You don't need any specialized training. All you need to do is step outside of yourself long enough to smile at someone and make the effort to let him know how you feel about seeing him.

He Welcomes the Unfaithful

But what if you haven't loved God faithfully? What if you have held something else to be more precious than Jesus, even to the point of abandoning him for it? What kind of attitude does he hold out if you want to return? Should you expect joyful, beaming gladness . . . or the stern demeanor of a sour vice principal? The story of the prodigal son lays bare God's longing for his children who have preferred the delights of reckless living to the pleasure of his company. Is there any more powerful image of welcome than one that shouts "I'm so glad you're back"?

We all knew Jake was in a dark place. Each guy in the support group had called or sent messages to him repeatedly for a month— all of which had gone unanswered. He was wrestling with his demons . . . again . . . and shutting everybody out . . . again. Then abruptly, he showed up one night. Sheepishly he talked about where he'd been and what he'd been doing.

And the guys were great. There were no recriminations about where he'd been or why he hadn't called. He heard light teasing that let him know he was accepted. But he also heard, "Hey, man! It's good to see you." "I'm just glad you're here tonight." "Thanks for sharing all that—that couldn't have been easy."

I heard the Father in their voices—the one who throws aside his dignity in a headlong dash down the road to welcome us back. You'd think a celebrity had come to town and was there waiting to sign autographs. Far from it. But the Father doesn't care. He wraps his arms around a young man who wasted his entire inheritance. A man who, although nurtured in his Father's house, had preferred his Father's cash to his company. And the Father doesn't object. He's simply thrilled to have his child back.

That was God's attitude toward you when you returned. He didn't even wait until you'd managed to climb all the way back to his house. Instead, he sprinted to where you were to embrace you. Could you imagine a greeting that would better communicate how welcome you are? The only one that tops this storybook version is the real one you have already personally experienced from your God.

Work your way through the Scripture and you will be amazed at how personal, enthusiastic, and welcoming your God is. Greeting people well is a God thing.

You Can Learn to Greet People Well

Greeting people well can be difficult because we're not born knowing how to do it. I know that firsthand, having practiced it badly over the years. I'm embarrassed to admit that when I started working in a counseling office, I used to enter the waiting room and invite a person back to my office with a clumsy, "Hi, Janine, how are you?"

Note to beginning counselors: in general, people coming for counseling aren't doing very well. Being asked publicly how they are does not improve how they're doing. It starts things off with an additional level of awkwardness, not to mention starting them off with a lie to hide themselves—"Um, I'm fine."

When you greet people, you indicate to them how worthwhile you think they are. The words you choose, the pose of your body, and your facial expression all communicate what you think of the other. Thankfully, the skill of greeting people is something you can learn.

Greeting someone well requires that you simultaneously pay

attention to (1) the person, including her life circumstances, and (2) the location of your meeting. You can ask a question in one scenario and have it understood as caring, if the person feels safe and protected. The same question would be horribly embarrassing and uncomfortable in a public setting where he feels exposed.

A family I know had a difficult fourth child. She was incredibly active all the time. She seemed to constantly push the envelope and regularly be in trouble. Her parents had taken to calling her "the little monster."

It seemed like a harmless, cute nickname—and rather appropriate. But they began to realize that as they addressed her that way, those half-kidding comments were revealing their own hearts and shaping their view of her. Ultimately, those words would determine their daughter's view of how others saw her. They repented by choosing nicknames that would publicly cherish her, not belittle her. They weren't being unreasonably optimistic—they still saw and understood her—but they wanted their greetings to communicate that they valued their daughter, not put her down.

When you see only someone's bad side, how do you get motivated to greet him differently? You learn to give people the time, energy, and experience that matches their worth and value. "But wait a minute!" I hear you saying. "That's just the problem. I don't have 'little monsters.' I have big ones. And I don't think they're worth the time or the trouble to greet well." Believe me, I have those people in my life too. Actually, if I'm honest, I probably am one of those monsters.

Value People Over Projects

It's been helpful for me to meditate on where Jesus says you will find true lasting value on this earth. He just finished helping his disciples see the foolishness of running after possessions like the people around them, when he gave a summary.

"Fear not, little flock, for it is your Father's good pleasure to give you the kingdom. Sell your possessions, and give to the needy. Provide yourselves with moneybags that do not grow old, with a treasure in the heavens that does not fail, where no thief approaches and no moth destroys. For where your treasure is, there will your heart be also." (Luke 12:32–34)

Moving them 180 degrees away from worrying about what they need to get, he urges them to sell their possessions and give to the poor. He tells them that this is the way to ensure treasure in heaven that no one can steal and that will not erode or decay.

As you reflect on what he says, you may realize that nothing on this earth lasts for eternity—except people. It follows that the only activities that will have enduring value are those you do for the sake of other eternal beings. Other people, then, are *the* most important part of your life today.

You have not met any ordinary people today—only eternal creatures made in God's image. That means from the first moment you lay eyes on someone, you need to respond in a way that communicates the value, worth, and dignity of the other that come from the status of being a forever-person.

You pause in what you're doing because you want the other person to know she is more important to you than things that will at some point decay or be stolen. You welcome her with an attitude that says "You belong here! I am so glad to know you. It's a privilege for us to have you here with us!" When you communicate that message, you set a tone for the rest of your interaction with the other person that embraces rather than pushes her away.

So many times people communicate with their greeting that others

So many times people communicate with their greeting that others are an imposition to what would otherwise be a smooth-running day.

are an imposition to what would otherwise be a smooth-running day. They barely look up, put on a forced smile that doesn't rise to the level of their eyes, or might even sigh when told someone has dropped by. That lack of greeting tells the other person he's not wanted.

Years ago I was challenged by a pastor's attitude about people dropping by unannounced. He and his staff had discussed the ways that people interrupted their days and kept them from getting to the things they planned to do. To help keep their priorities straight, this pastor helped his staff realize "People are not an interruption to the ministry; people *are* the ministry." That's an important principle to live by, whether you're working in a church setting or not.

My neighbor and I joke that we can't work around the yard without attracting people who want to stop and talk. That feels like an interruption when you have a project you just want to wrap up. But when viewed from the perspective of eternity—that only people are going to last—those "interruptions" are actually divine opportunities to connect with an eternal soul who embodies unlimited value.

That changes how I engage people when they drop by as I'm shoveling mulch. Before I look up, I need to

> "People are not an interruption to the ministry; people are the ministry."

think about what my first words and actions will communicate. Will my friends understand that they are important or that they are inconvenient? Will I invite them to share themselves or to move along?

True, there are times when you find yourself backed against a wall with other commitments and time constraints that won't allow you to be interrupted to the degree someone would like. It is possible, however, to believe that people come before projects without giving them permission to absorb your life. How you communicate that to them is important. It is far too easy to send subtle messages and hints hoping they will see you'd like them to go away.

There was a time when I served both as the pastor of counseling for one church and interim pastor of another congregation that had asked for help. People would drop by my office and ask, "Are you busy?" I'm helping pastor two congregations along with caring for my family and their needs . . . am I busy? Of course I am, and I'm supposed to be, but I'm not so busy that I can't be interrupted. How do I learn to communicate that? Mostly by making mistakes.

Tyler dropped by and asked if I was busy. You've had that happen to you, haven't you? Someone comes by your office when you have a project deadline quickly approaching. Or you're home trying to get dinner ready or hurrying to race out the door to soccer practice when the phone rings and someone wants to know if you have time to talk. I hesitated before answering Tyler that afternoon. Then I invited him in, but didn't get up to greet him or try hard to carry the conversation. After a very uncomfortable ten minutes, during which I was clearly distracted, he took the hint and excused himself.

Thankfully, I felt convicted by my refusal to love him, so that when—amazingly—he dropped by several months later, I did stop what I was doing, invite him in, and actively engage him in conversation. However, I was even busier that time. So after fifteen minutes I honestly let him know that I was sorry, but I had some other things I needed to get to. We parted on much better terms because we'd had a real connection.

Welcoming someone well doesn't mean you surrender everything to his or her agenda. It means you make time to share your life at that moment, and if you can't spare much, you make arrangements to connect again at a later time.

Become Intentional

A few years back my wife reentered the work force, which meant that several days a week I was the one who would be home for the kids when school was out. I knew I needed to create a welcoming atmosphere for them, but I also knew it would be difficult for me.

Have you ever worked from home? I am so aware of what I need to get done *and* so distracted by things in the house that I am really tempted to slight the people around me and give them only part of my attention while I desperately try to get something accomplished. Thankfully, I realized that trying to multitask when the kids returned would not communicate how much I valued and wanted them.

So the moment they opened the outside door, I made a point to immediately put my pen down. I turned away from the table with my papers and computer on it so I could face whoever was in the room. Intentionally I smiled at them and said something like "Welcome home! I am really glad to see you!" We'd hug and then with the time I had planned to set aside, I asked, "So, how was your day?" and really listened.

You have to make your body agree with what your mouth is saying. If there's a mismatch, people will conclude that your words are not as true as your actions lead them to believe. If someone comes to visit you and you can't be bothered to pause, turn, and at least look at her, she will (and should) conclude that she's not very important to you. If the TV, video game, vacuuming, or book is too important for you to interrupt to welcome your family and friends, then they rightly understand that they have lost some of their importance to you. Your outside actions always reflect your inner priorities. That means you have to greet with your whole body, not just with a few scattered words.

You Will Have to Work Hard

If you're thinking, *That sounds like a lot of work*, you're right. It is. Valuing people always takes effort. Because of the fall of humanity into sin, I am so radically self-absorbed that I don't even know it. What comes *naturally* for me is to consider my own comforts above the needs of other people.

I still remember the time I "counseled" a thirteen-year-old boy. It was a painful experience for both of us. He was reluctant to talk, and I had no idea how to connect with him. As the session went on, I sat back in my chair more and more, covered my mouth with my hand, and progressively matched his slouch. We got quieter and quieter until I'm surprised one of us didn't nod off. I did not create an environment that welcomed him.

What made it even more agonizing for me was that my supervisor had wanted me to videotape the session so that he could review my technique. I knew it was not going to be any fun for him to watch, but I hadn't expected him to fast-forward through so much of it. He was very gentle in his comments as he pointed out that I was "a little flat."

He then told a story of how he had been getting ready to teach a class of counseling students. Someone mentioned to him later that he had come in more energized than usual. As my mentor thought about that experience he realized that he had been more engaged with the material because he was thinking ahead of time about how people needed it, and that realization had a positive effect on his teaching style. His focus on the people altered his presentation without his awareness.

He helped me recognize that I needed to pick up my energy level when relating to other people for *their* sake. When counseling, I needed to sit up and sit forward. I needed to smile and work hard to be engaged. I couldn't afford to let myself simply drift with the flow. I had to intentionally communicate to the other person that I was glad he was there.

The same is true for my regular relationships—and it is for you too. It takes real work to create a warm, inviting atmosphere.

Greeting people well is completely in line with the gospel of grace. Romans 15:7 says, "Welcome one another as Christ has welcomed you, for the glory of God." Jesus reaches out to undeserving people and makes sure you and I know we are welcomed home. His attitude gives us confidence that he will receive us, and his attitude continues to draw us. That's the same attitude we offer to others when we greet them. If you find that you too easily hold people at arm's length, it's time to reexperience the God who is happy to see you.

On Your Own

1. Study how God greets people in the Bible. Write down what you learn. Make a list of times that quickly come to your mind. Then flip through the pages in your Bible looking for other instances. You may even want to ask your friends if they can remember any episodes of greeting in the Bible. Then look at what God says and how he approaches people. What do you see?

2. What signals do you send that communicate disinterest to others? If you're not sure, be bold and ask someone what he's noticed about your greetings. It could be anything from your demeanor to the words you use or how you hold your body.

3. Prayerfully ask God why you don't greet others well. What do you find more engaging or interesting? While you're in prayer, ask him to allow you to more fully experience his greeting and the enthusiasm he has to be with you.

4. Consider the people in your life with whom you need to be more welcoming. Maybe it's a family member, roommate, friend, or

neighbor. Give yourself a definite time period to intentionally work at greeting that person well each time you come in contact with him or her. Think about what you will do and say differently. Afterward, evaluate what has happened in you personally and in your relationship.

CHAPTER 12

Humble Love: Submitting to Each Other

Humility is necessary whenever you try to blend two or more lives together. To successfully bring together different personalities, likes, and interests, you need to be practiced at humility. Even if it's only for a short time or a limited project—an evening out with friends, renovations at home, dividing weekly cleaning chores, a missions trip—humility is a necessary ingredient.

This chapter looks at humble love, learning to bend yourself around what someone else needs from you. It makes relating possible while the opposite, insisting that others get in line with your viewpoint, will keep you disconnected from the people around you.

As hard as it is to comprehend, humility on God's part underlies his relationship with you. You see that in the way he stoops to serve you, doing for you what you never could do for yourself. But you also see it in the way he relates to you as he invites you to bring your thoughts and concerns to him as a friend, rather than slavishly supplicate an arrogant deity who holds himself above you.

You, in turn, treat your friends with the same kind of submissive love that doesn't demand they meet you on your terms. Rather, you now gladly work to cross over to them. This is a beautiful gift to give the people around you, but it is generally not pictured as attractive in our world. Few of us tend to associate positive images with words like "humility" and "submission."

For instance, one memorable scene from the miniseries version of James Clavell's *Shogun* comes early in the film. John Blackthorne, an English mariner from the seventeenth century, is shipwrecked on the island of Japan. Appalled at the treatment accorded to him and his fellow sailors and the subsequent Japanese demands, he blurts out to Omi (the head captor) words of extreme disrespect to Omi and Japan.

In response, Omi orders one of Blackthorne's crewmen to be boiled alive. To prevent this atrocity, Blackthorne pledges himself to obey all of Omi's commands without question or hesitation. To drive the lesson home, Omi orders Blackthorne to lie facedown on the ground and proceeds to relieve himself on Blackthorne's back. Clearly Blackthorne is submitting to the other man. But just as clearly, his submission is forced, having more to do with humiliation than humility. It is *completely* unattractive.

Isn't that the case with most of the pictures you have of submission? For many people, the word "submit" conjures images of playground bullies, abusive husbands, narcissistic friends, repressive parents, dictatorial employers, unfair law enforcement officers, or uncaring government bureaucracies. At the very least it sounds like you lose part of your personality as you come under the influence of someone else. Even worse, you lose the freedom to make your own decisions. Or, worst of all, you lose your dignity as someone forces you to do something against your will.

In our society, submission doesn't have many positive connotations. I have yet to meet the child who says, "Oh, I just can't wait to grow up so that I can submit to someone else!" For many children it's just the opposite. They can't wait to grow up because they think they won't have to listen to *anyone* anymore.

One day I was trying to help my son see that even after he leaves my house he will still have to listen to lots of people in life—professors, coaches, police, employers, and government, to name a few. I pointed out that even if he found some way to opt out of listening to other humans—purchase his own island?—he'd still need to listen to God. No one ever gets out of learning to submit himself to someone else. It's funny, but none of my kids have ever gotten excited by that revelation.

Partly this is because they are born with unwillingness and partly it stems from a lack of positive role models (myself included, no doubt) that make humility attractive. Thankfully, the situation is not hopeless. When you have trouble thinking of an engaging example of what God calls you to grow in, consider where you see it in Jesus.

Jesus Submitted First

Paul the apostle summarizes a Jesus-style humility in his letter to the Philippians.

> In humility count others more significant than yourself. Let each of you look not only to his own interests, but also to the interests of others. Have this mind among yourselves, which is yours in Christ Jesus, who, though he was in the form of God, did not count equality with God a thing to be grasped, but made himself nothing, taking the form of a servant, being born in the likeness of men. And being found in human form, he humbled himself by becoming obedient to the point of death, even death on a cross. (Philippians 2:3–8)

God is an amazing union of extremes. I cannot think of anyone in a higher position, with more power, who has enjoyed more beauty in the context of better relationships. There isn't anyone more privileged than God. Yet at the same moment, I cannot think of anyone who has given up more. He left it all behind—power, beauty, peace, relationships—to embrace their polar opposites of physical weaknesses, tense relationships, suffering, abuse, torture, physical death, and spiritual torment.

Why did he give up so much? Because he was literally unwilling to consider eternity without you. He was not forced into humility against his will to appease someone's longing for power or to meet some deep neediness in himself. He voluntarily gave up his rights and privileges so your life and mine would be better. Your Lord and Master did not organize his world according to what would be most comfortable and enjoyable for himself. Instead, he altered his world to benefit you.

> You're allowed to have your own interests, but they are not to rule your life. Instead, you are to reshape your world for the sake of someone else.

Not surprisingly, Jesus invites you to learn the joy of humbling yourself for others' sake by following his example. Now you get to live with others in a way that thinks about their needs more than you think of your own. You're allowed to have your own interests, but they are not to rule your life. Instead, you are to reshape your world for the sake of someone else.

That's a hard calling, but it is one that fosters healthy relationships as you work to involve yourself in someone else's world rather than hold yourself aloof from him. Thankfully, in laying down his privileges, Jesus gives you one that you might not have expected: He gives you the same mind that he has. He puts inside of you a new way to think about yourself in relationship to other people.

Submitting Is a Mark of the Spirit's Work

Active, attractive humility is so important for the Christian that it's the central hinge of Paul's letter to the Ephesians. This aspect of love is so important that if you don't understand it and live it out, you are missing a crucial piece of what it is to know Christ in his family. Look at this passage from the middle of the book.

> And do not get drunk with wine, for that is debauchery, but be filled with the Spirit, addressing one another in psalms and hymns and spiritual songs, singing and making melody to the Lord with all your heart, giving thanks always and for everything to God the Father in the name of our Lord Jesus Christ, submitting to one another out of reverence for Christ. Wives, submit to your own husbands, as to the Lord. (Ephesians 5:18–22)

Follow the logic here to see how essential submitting is to the way we live with each other. In the Greek for this verse, the word "submitting" is actually a participle, which means it doesn't stand on its own but helps explain another verb in the sentence. To find that verb, you have to work backward to verse 18, where you are commanded to be filled by the Holy Spirit. Submitting to each other, then, is one of the evidences that you have received the Spirit of the living God. That means that verse 21 is necessarily attached to verse 18.

But verse 21 also connects with what comes next. If you look at verse 22 you'll read, "Wives, submit to your own husbands, as to the Lord." Your version of the Bible might italicize "submit." Now husbands, please don't get excited—the italics are not there to show Paul's emphasis, as though he was making sure the ladies really got the point. Instead, the italics help you realize that word is not present in the best Greek manuscripts.

Verse 22 reads literally: "Wives to your own husbands, as to the Lord." It's a phrase that takes the previous verb form as its own and it depends on the participle for its meaning.[1] Therefore, "Wives, submit to your husbands," is the correct English translation, but that means that verse 22 flows from verse 21, tying those two together.

When you realize that verse 21 goes with verse 22, you understand it is connected to the next three sections as well. These sections describe different kinds of relationships you might have in the church: 5:22–33 discusses wives and husbands relating to each other; 6:1–4 refers to children and fathers getting along; and 6:5–9 talks about the relationship between masters and slaves.

The command to submit to each other is both part of verse 18 as well as an introduction to the longer section that follows. In that sense, verse 21 is the connecting link between being filled with the Holy Spirit and living well in the community of faith, making it the focal point of the book.

Submitting yourself to others becomes the primary distinguishing mark of how you live in the family. You take your plans, your interests, your likes, your dislikes, your agendas, and your preferences and you make them of secondary importance to what other family members need from you. Not because you're afraid of what they might think about you if you don't or because you need them to like you, but out of genuine concern for their best interests. You accommodate yourself to what is good for your friends.

I came home from a full day of counseling feeling a bit schizophrenic. In rapid succession I'd played the role of a wise, older uncle with a young married couple; a sarcastic, needling skeptic with a teenage male; and a sympathetic, if somewhat detached, professional with another couple. As I wondered whether I was just a hypocritical chameleon, I thought about my motivation. I wasn't changing my approach to ingratiate myself with anyone or to benefit personally, but so that I could reach them where they were and help them. In that sense, I think I was following Paul's example of becoming all things to all people (1 Corinthians 9:22). His is an example of radical submission.

Becoming what someone else needs me to be never ends. I went home that day and had more opportunities to shape myself around other people's interests: as husband, partner, father, homework tutor, friend, disciplinarian, sports coach, guide, flirtatious lover, animal trainer, maid, and repairman—in short, what different individuals needed me to be. I never stop being who I am, but what that looks like at any given moment depends both on who is in front of me and what that person needs. Submissive love does not come in a one-size-fits-all package.

Take a moment to think about the two or three closest relationships you have. What do those people need to experience from you? What parts of your personality would be helpful for you to express with them more fully? Which parts do you need to resist emphasizing for their sake?

Two General Guidelines for Submission

It is easy to swing your life between two bad approaches to submission: refusing to bend around another person's needs unless you feel like it or believing you are required to do what everyone else wants you to. Neither of those polar opposites embodies the spirit of Christian humility. Here are a few guidelines to help you distinguish godly humility from dysfunctional codependency and rampant selfishness.

First, remember that godly submission is not a fifty–fifty proposition. You don't put in half the effort while the other person contributes the rest. Nor is it a conditional arrangement, where you submit your will and agenda so long as you think the other is going to as well. Your submission to others grows out of your reverence for Christ, not reverence for other people. That allows you to carry out your calling to put the other's best interests ahead of your own, regardless of who that person is, 100 percent of the time.

> *Your submission to others grows out of your reverence for Christ, not reverence for other people.*

This next guideline guards you from unwittingly creating more brokenness. Always remember that, in a loving relationship, no one calls the shots all the time. While the first guideline urges you to give all you've got in relationships, the second guards you from reinforcing someone else's dysfunctional relational patterns.

Have you ever had a relationship in which you could not cross the other person? Someone who with her words or attitudes essentially said, "It's my way or the highway"? Where the person threatened to take away any relational connection unless you always agreed with her in most things, if not everything? That person is not living a lifestyle of submission. Someone who cannot receive input, hear a rebuke, or consider doing something differently than what she planned is not a person who submits to others.

In this context, it is remarkable to consider that Jesus, the person who always knew what was best, allowed people to alter his plans. Do you remember how he began traveling to a centurion's house to heal his servant? Then the centurion sent someone to say, "I'm unworthy to have you in my home." Jesus stopped and healed the man's servant without continuing to the man's home (Luke 7:1–10). Surely the centurion was humble, but notice that so was Jesus as he adjusted his plan according to what he heard.

Or how about the time when the Syrophoenician woman wanted him to heal her daughter? Jesus told her it wasn't right to take the children's food and throw it to the dogs. But instead of walking away, taking his response as final, she respectfully challenged him by saying that even the dogs got the children's scraps. Jesus answered her by saying, "For this statement"—her challenge to what Jesus said to her!—"you may go your way; the demon has left your daughter" (Mark 7:24–30).

God invites people to talk to him after he's planned what he's going to do. And on several occasions, he modifies his plans based on conversations with his people.[2] Somehow those modifications fit into the plans he already had for his people from the beginning of time. I don't claim to know how that works, but I do know that he doesn't shut people down when they disagree with him. There's a huge element of humility in God. If that's how your relationship with God works, why would you hope for anything less than mutual respect from your human relationships?

If you have a relationship that is one-sided, one in which the other person is in sole control of the direction and flow of the relationship, then that person is not demonstrating the evidence of a Spirit-filled life. And that relationship is not the kind that God has planned for the people in his family.

Situations like this are too complex and often too volatile for a couple of quick pointers to fix them. To give advice I need to know you, the other person, and have a sense of how your relationship has gotten to this place. Having said that, an early pre-step would be to locate someone *safe* to whom you could confide honestly that your relationship is one-sided. You would not do this to gossip or slander, but as the beginning step of enlisting help to discover what specific steps wisdom would take in your position.

At some point, you will need to let the other person know that you're not okay with the present state of your relationship. This is an application of pursuing love (Chapter 7) and the section "Healthy Relationships Gently Confront" (Chapter 8) that we talked about earlier.

You need to be motivated by a concern for the danger the other person has put himself into. That danger might take the form of arrogantly thinking he doesn't need anyone's help. Or it might look more like he feels too insecure to engage in a partnership he doesn't completely control. Whatever the case, it is not good for him to continue living in a one-sided relationship and believe that it is healthy.

Once you point out the problem, you want to invite him or her to work toward relating differently, while having a contingency plan of retreating to a safe place in case this person is unwilling to work toward something different. That plan needs to be guided by someone who has experience (for example, a pastor or counselor) and needs to be carried out within a larger community (for example, friends or a close fellowship group) that can help support you both emotionally as well as physically.

A Guideline for Those Who Lead

This third guideline reminds you explicitly that even those in positions of authority are called to submit to those they lead. You see this clearly as Paul works through relationships in the book of Ephesians. He specifically calls people, who in that culture would have thought they were exempt from humbling themselves, to submit to the less powerful partner. Husbands, you don't get to have everything you want—you are to die for your wife's sake. Fathers, you don't get to say and do whatever you feel like with your kids—you may not frustrate them. Masters, you are not the absolute authority in your businesses—you too have a master over you.[3]

Submitting yourself to others is for every Christian in every relationship in every time and every place. Regardless of what position I am in, whether I'm the one in authority or under someone else's authority, I have a calling from Christ to humble myself before others for their benefit.

For the person in authority this means not pushing your own agenda as though God has spoken only through you. You don't lord it over other people. Instead, you learn to listen to them. You welcome input and others letting you know how they feel about the direction you're trying to take them. That means you'll probably need to invite them to speak up.

When my assistant first came to work with us, I thought she might be hesitant to give me her input. We had four strikes against us. She was from the respectful South while I was reared in the less-respectful North. I had been her professor at seminary, and I also had more counseling experience than she had. Additionally, we were dealing with the male-female dynamic (I've had several ladies point out that, in mixed gender settings, men will feel relatively free to volunteer their ideas, while women tend to hold back, waiting to be invited).

These four things made me wonder whether she'd be comfortable speaking her mind. If she wasn't, it would not be good for her, the counseling center, or me. So after her first week, while we were debriefing how things were going, I said to her, "Okay, here's a question that we're regularly going to come back to. I don't expect you to have an answer today, but it's a question that's always on the table so you need to get used to it: How am I making your job or life difficult? What am I doing that frustrates you?"

She didn't have much of a response . . . then. But she has come back since with thoughts that have been really healthy and good because that's the kind of invitation that sticks with a person. If you're in a position of authority, part of submitting to others involves inviting them to give their input.

Which of your places of leadership can you invite people to give their input? This is not only for work-related relationships. I learned to ask the question about making someone's life difficult from a man who asked it of his wife. I, in turn, have asked it at home and gotten great feedback that has made our family life better. It helps us in the moment as I hear where people struggle to live with me and I work to make things easier on them. But it also helps us long-term by setting a tone in our household that says "I want to hear from you how you experience living with me."

Think carefully. Who in your life needs to hear you ask these kinds of humble, submissive questions?

Every person in leadership—whether in the church or home—needs to honor others, serve others, hear from others, respect others, and adjust their plans based on input. But that doesn't mean that a leader stops leading. A leader who submits to others is far different from someone who is a people-pleaser. How do you know the difference between a servant-leader and someone who only wants people to be happy with him? A true servant makes decisions that give people what they need, which is not always the same as what they want.

Anyone can promise you everything you've always wanted—and some people can even make that happen, for awhile. But someone who truly loves you, who is most interested in you and in your good, is someone who is willing to forego his or her own happiness to make sure you have what you need. A submissive leader doesn't ask, "What will bring *me* the best results?" but is concerned instead with, "What will most benefit the people around me?"

A Guideline for Those Who Are Being Led

Leaders have to learn to submit if they're going to lead well, but so do those who are being led. This last guideline invites those who do not have a leadership position in the relationship to gladly, joyfully take someone else's direction . . . with a couple of caveats.

You willingly follow when that direction does not violate Christ's call on your life. Make sure you keep that last phrase from Ephesians 5:21 in mind: submitting to one another out of reverence for Christ. You submit yourself to others *out of reverence for Christ.* That means you can follow someone else only so long as he does not lead you to sin against God.

Now some people might use that as an excuse to make their leader's lives miserable, demanding chapter and verse for every decision before they'll move. That's not a submissive attitude. Leaders need to make sure they're *in line* with God's desires, and people under their authority need to make sure the leaders are *not out of line* with God's desires. That means if it's not clearly sinful, there needs to be an attitude in you that says, "If that's the way you want to do it, then that's the way I'm going to do it."

I've been learning this better over the last year. My lead pastor asked me to write a letter that we would send to the congregation. I didn't think it was the best thing we could do, but after hearing my input, he still thought it was what we should do. So my response at that point was, "Absolutely. I'll get right on it." I went back to my office and fit it into my schedule that day. Submission to one another when there is no sin involved starts to approach the idea of "Your wish becomes my command." I don't have to be ordered or commanded. Instead, I learn to willingly, gladly do what you've asked me to.

But did you also hear how part of submitting to someone else involves learning to speak up appropriately? There are two easy errors you can fall into. On one side, you can demand to be heard. You assume it's your right to say whatever you want to say and that the other person has to be willing to hear you. "I might have to submit to you, but you're going to know exactly what I'm thinking and how I'm feeling." That's a very American attitude—but not a very Christian one.

Perhaps you're on the opposite extreme: you figure a truly

submissive person wouldn't speak up, that you don't have a place to do so, or maybe it's just easier that way. You think, *If I speak up then I might get blasted so it's better just to keep my head down and do what I'm told.* That's also a very understandable response— and also not very Christian.

Neither demanding to speak nor believing you can't seeks to give your best to someone else. In that sense, neither one is Christlike submission. These responses show either a lack of self-control or a lack of boldness. Neither one requires the Holy Spirit and both sell your redemption short.

When you submit yourself to others out of reverence for Christ (Ephesians 5:21), you are doing so because that is what is best for all the people involved. That means Jesus has given you responsibility for each other, which requires you to speak up at times. Sometimes you will offer your ideas as a better alternative to what the other person thinks. Other times you'll speak up because it's not good for the other person to treat you the way he is.

Your calling to be submissive is not a calling to be less present or active in the relationship, like some dutiful robot or animal. It's not a call to pretend you have no ideas or wisdom of your own, to always go along with whatever someone else decides. Those are abuses of submission. When you abuse submission, you allow someone else to abuse her authority. Out of reverence for Christ, you cannot go along with that dynamic.

This is such a difficult thing to live out that it should bring you to your knees in godly desperation. That brings us full circle to verse 18 of Ephesians 5, where instead of filling yourself with the creation, you are to be filled with the Creator. Without the active, ongoing filling of the Holy Spirit, you will never be able to submit yourself to anyone in a way that benefits and helps another. Instead, you will keep you and others immature.

This is a glorious command, but one that you can only fill if the Lord empowers you. So ask him to humbly serve you one more time by filling you with himself so that you can put others' interests ahead of your own.

On Your Own

1. What makes it hard for you to submit? A demand to have your own way, to make your life easy or comfortable? A fear of being hurt or run over? Unattractive pictures in your mind or experiences from your past? When you are stuck and unwilling to submit to others, how does Jesus' submission to you for your sake help you get unstuck?

2. Meditate on Jesus' humility. Do you regularly see God come to rescue you despite your unworthiness? What does it feel like to be that sought after? When was the last time you told him you appreciate what he's done?

3. Quiz your friends about times when they didn't demand their own way, but bent themselves to someone else's needs for the other's sake. What was that like for them? Why did they do it? How was it hard? How did they experience Jesus through it? Where did they see God's glory shine through?

4. To whom do you have the hardest time submitting—your friends, spouse, parents, neighbors, children, supervisor, employee? What are the next steps Jesus invites you to take?

CHAPTER 13

Celebrating Love: Rejoicing with Each Other

In a healthy relationship, you are able to rejoice with your friends in their good fortune. She feels comfortable telling you the good things in her life and you respond by being genuinely glad for her.

In this chapter we're looking at celebrating love, an aspect of loving well that affects your relationships in two ways. First, it removes the strain between people that develops when one is unsure how his good news will be received so he keeps it secret from the other. Second, you give the other person greater confidence in the friendship because she realizes you are not trying to use her. Far from wanting what she has, you rejoice with her that she has it.

This kind of love flows out of the way God celebrates his friendship with you. He doesn't squeeze you dry, trying to see how much he can get from you. Instead, he gives you gifts that suit your needs, both physical and nonphysical, then invites you to see beyond the gift to himself. In that process, you have the opportunity to see how much better the Giver is than any of his gifts.

That same dynamic takes place when God blesses your friends.

You can love them by rejoicing with them that he has cared about them and also shown you more of his nature in what he gave. At first glance, this doesn't seem like it would be too hard to do. But it can be.

Rejoicing with Others Can Be Hard

When my son plays with his kitten, his smile, laughter, and joy are infectious. They travel across the room more surely and quickly than any cold germ, and I instinctively smile as I catch his joy. Why would God have to command me to "rejoice with those who rejoice" (Romans 12:15)? When my wife is happy with her hairstyle, I'm happy. When my daughter proudly shows me her test score, the words "way to go!" easily roll off my lips. Rejoicing with those who rejoice seems easy.

There are times, however, when those words come much more slowly, like when my colleague gets the promotion I'd been hoping for—the one I thought I deserved because I had worked harder, been there longer, and made greater sacrifices. Suddenly it's not so easy to rejoice with those who rejoice. Can you rejoice when:

- your husband starts to have friends who call him and spend time with him, even though you can't remember the last time the two of you talked?
- the guy you were interested in asks your roommate out?
- your friend announces she's about to have her seventh grandchild and your kids haven't even gotten married?
- your neighbors fly to Bermuda for vacation while you journey to the township swimming pool?
- the woman in your fellowship group "accidentally" got pregnant while you're taking fertility drugs that only make you feel cranky—and poor?

- your brother-in-law shows off his new iPhone, 52" high-def flat screen TV, minivan, interactive videogame station, apartment, house, and so on?
- your noncommunicative daughter wins the "Citizen of the Month" award at school even though she mostly keeps herself locked inside her room at home?

Maybe rejoicing with those who rejoice is not always easy. It's harder to be happy for you when my desires enter into the picture. Instead of focusing on you and your joy, my mind wanders to me and how much I would like to have what you got.

That's the root, isn't it, when I refuse to rejoice with you or force myself to act happy for you? I am thinking of what I didn't get. The three most common varieties of this are covetousness, jealousy, and envy. *Covetousness* focuses on the things someone else owns and says "I want what you have!" *Jealousy* doesn't focus on things, but on a person, and proclaims "I want to have you!" *Envy* takes your dissatisfaction with your own life almost to a pathological self-hatred: "I want to be you!" Covetousness, jealousy, and envy are three expressions of the belief that "If there were any justice in the world, what you have should belong to me. Somehow, somewhere, there's been a mistake and you got what I deserve."

You and I know that attitude poisons any relationship it touches. It clearly signals to the other that the relationship is one-sided. No doubt you've seen its effects on the people around you. Why then do we keep falling into it if it's so visibly destructive?

Lies Keep Me from Rejoicing with You

There are several lies that make covetousness, jealousy, and envy easy to fall into and attractive to our hearts. First, I am deeply convinced that temporal things are completely satisfying and that if only I had what you do, I would no longer feel incomplete or unhappy. It's crazy that I fool myself into thinking that the next accomplishment or acquisition will satisfy me, despite all the evidence to the contrary. I forget how each previous purchase, each rung on the ladder of accomplishment that I climbed, was nice only for a season. I forget how quickly the luster of each one dimmed, prompting me to reset my sights on acquiring something else. Concerned with getting ahead myself, I become, at best, blinded to how good it is for you to be blessed. At worst, I become resentful of your good fortune.

The second lie that keeps me from rejoicing with you is that temporal things are randomly, chaotically distributed across the universe. When I will not rejoice with my friends, I express my belief that God is not involved in dispersing gifts as he desires and thinks best. Instead, I let myself live within what amounts to an atheistic worldview, believing that everything that happens is a series of disconnected events without any rhyme, reason, or purpose.

In other words, refusing to rejoice with others is the equivalent of being trapped inside a life-long Monopoly game. I hate Monopoly. In my experience, it is a three-hour exercise in slowly watching someone else prosper by my increasing poverty, based almost entirely on chance. "Oh, look! I accidentally rolled a nine and now I owe you bazillions of dollars because earlier you accidentally rolled a three and were able to purchase hotels." In this Monopoly-mindset I have no control over my fate or the rewards or the consequences that come to me—and neither does anyone else. It's all based on blind luck without overarching purpose or meaning. One of us gets everything while everyone else steadily loses everything. And I take it personally. Inside I seethe, *This isn't fair!*

If that's the world I live in, why should I rejoice when you roll a good number, pick up a "Get Out of Jail Free" card, or are magically told to move to the third property you needed to create an unbeat-able monopoly? Rejoice with you? Hah! I'll grumble, curse your luck, believe the universe is against me, or get discouraged and quit. If that's the world I live in, rejoicing doesn't make any sense.

Rejoicing over the goodness you experienced only makes sense in a different world. One that is not random or chaotic. One in which gifts are distributed with order, purpose, and meaning be-cause there is an Order-er, Purpose-er, and Meaning-maker.

There is a third lie that keeps me from celebrating with you: I wrongly believe this life is the only life my appetites and desires can find satisfaction in. When I am filled with covetousness, envy, and jealousy, I do not allow myself to consider that there might be greater satisfaction apart from what I have and hold. Instead, I functionally believe that my passions and longings must find their ultimate fulfillment in physical things and accomplishments.

By forgetting that I was made for more than this life, it only makes sense to set my heart on obtaining all I can while I'm here. That means that if you happen to have more than I do, I will not be able to freely support you in the goodness that you enjoy. I will taint our relationship with my longings for what you have, even if those desires go unspoken.

In those moments, I believe that temporal things are an end in themselves. I don't see them as attached to anything greater, and I don't realize that they always point back to the One who gave them. I miss that the good things you have are small tastes of God's gener-ous concern for his people.

I forget that the gift, no matter how great it is, is always smaller and less good than God is himself. And so I act out my belief that I cannot be happy and content unless I have the gift. The Giver is nice, but he is not enough.

When you believe these lies, it makes sense that you would not rejoice with others over their gifts. And yet, as evil as your reluctance is, it can become the catalyst to learning celebration as another way to love people.

The moment you become aware that you tend to hold back your joy from other people is the moment when you (re)discover that you're no longer moving outward to enjoy and embrace your friendships. Now you are able to see more clearly that you've fallen back into wanting your relationships to serve you. This is not a depressing, guilt-ridden moment. It's the necessary beginning step of reconnecting with the people around you as you grow more confident that God knows what he's doing when he gives things to other people that you wish he had given you.

Truths That Free Me to Rejoice with You

James reorients you to this path as he summarizes the relationship between God and his gifts with his usual directness: "Every good gift and every perfect gift is from above, coming down from the Father of lights with whom there is no variation or shadow due to change" (James 1:17). Three important implications that are antidotes to the lies we discussed flow from this verse.

First, gifts have an origin that is neither random nor chaotic. They come down to us from God, who claims throughout Scripture that he is intentional in the ways he deals with people. He distributes his good and perfect gifts exactly to the people he planned.

At Mardi Gras celebrations, gifts are given indiscriminately—beads, imitation coins, even stuffed animals are thrown haphazardly from floats into the awaiting crowds. People try to get the giver's attention by holding signs or dressing to attract enough attention to get the good stuff. But even if someone throws a prize in your direction, it doesn't mean you're guaranteed to get it. You will still have to grab it out of the air or maybe even dive for it on the street. God doesn't give his gifts that way. No one inadvertently intercepts them. He ensures they get to where they are supposed to go.

The second antidote is to realize these gifts are uniquely crafted to suit our individual requirements. Each of God's children is one of a kind, absolutely noninterchangeable. Therefore, for a gift to be good and perfect, it has to precisely match the needs of the person it was given to.

You know this from experience. Have you ever had someone give you a gift that so completely missed your tastes and needs that you knew from the moment you first saw it that you would never pick it up again? Contrast that with gifts that excited you because they exactly suited your taste and style. You realize that the person either knew you well or worked hard to learn about you. God's gifts are perfect because he knows exactly what you need and he gladly, graciously gives according to your needs.

> ... when I see you receive something good, I need to stop my knee-jerk "I didn't get any!" response to life. Instead, I need to remind myself that, in God's infinite wisdom, he decided that was exactly what you needed—which means it is exactly not what I need.

That's liberating news. When I realize that God makes his gifts fit each person, there's no way I can covet what you got because it just wouldn't fit me. It would be like me trying to wear the clothes of our 6' 4" elder. It doesn't matter how much I might like his style or how much I want to fill my closet, his clothes are just not going to fit me.

God's gifts are that specific as well. Being envious of you or desiring what you have misses the point that the things he's given you won't fit me. Instead of mass producing his gifts, God tailor fits every gift so that it is precisely right for the receiver.

Because of this when I see you receive something good, I need to stop my knee-jerk "I didn't get any!" response to life. Instead, I need to remind myself that, in God's infinite wisdom, he decided that was exactly what *you* needed—which means it is exactly *not* what I need. That truth will set you free, but it also calls for faith as you learn to trust that he knows what you need even more than you do.

The third antidote is to remember these gifts come "from the Father of lights with whom there is no variation or shadow due to change." They are personal, from your very good Father. As such, just like every other part of creation, they are an external expression of his inner essence—his personality, care, and concern. They tell you about him.

Whether I get the gift or you get the gift, we both have the opportunity to see our God more clearly because of it. Remembering that upward focus moves my eyes off you and me. I rejoice with you as I contemplate how he expressed his relationship with you. I concentrate on how he gave you *exactly* what you needed, how *careful* he was in choosing it, and how his *timing* was just right for you.

I also realize that his gifts are small tastes of things yet to come. God himself is the most glorious possession anyone could ever have. Therefore all the things around us are, at best, weak tastes of him. So when I see you get something good I rejoice with you, because in that good thing I see the promise of something better— I see him. And I know that both you and I will share in this better thing—God himself—together. Now I can be happy for you, not because I think less of your gift, but because I think more of the Giver.

Unfortunately that's often easier to say than to do. But thank God that even when you struggle to value him over his presents, he doesn't abandon you. In the moment when you can't seem to rejoice with others, the biggest, best gift God could ever offer you is the gift of himself. That's exactly the gift you need. You have made yourself sick and kept yourself from fully enjoying other people because you want things that can never fully satisfy you. What could he possibly give that would match your desperate condition perfectly? You need the gift of being set free from yourself and from longing for things that cannot satisfy.

To that end, the Giver of all good gifts gives you himself. You can have your soul satisfied even now because he will give you the gift of not being caught up in yourself. He will set you free from selfishness so you can rejoice with others. He could offer you no kinder thing in that moment when in your heart you hate the kindness he has shown to others. Therefore, in rejoicing with those who rejoice, we celebrate the kindness Jesus brought into our dark world.

And when I celebrate his kindness with you, I give you confidence that I'm your friend for reasons other than what I can get from you. Celebrating gives both of us greater confidence in our relationship.

Re-experiencing the Heart of Our Celebratory God

But what if you're not very good at celebrating? What if you don't do it very often, you don't feel like it much, or you don't really know how? If you don't know how to rejoice with the people around you, you have missed the overflowing, rejoicing heart of God.

You will learn to rejoice well with others only when you have seen that rejoicing and celebrating is a deep character trait of our God. It is part of how he loves his people. And it's an important characteristic he builds into all his people as they share their lives with each other.

Christians should be foremost among those who celebrate—because we already have so much more to rejoice about. Sadly, we've lost much of the emphasis on corporate rejoicing in the Western Protestant church. That loss affects our personal relationships because if our larger communities aren't marked by corporate celebration, there's little context for learning how to rejoice individually.

A friend of mine spent hours pouring grace into someone's life by saying to him over and over, "I am so sorry that people have represented God so badly to you." That person had grown up knowing God as a dour, nonrelational rule-giver. Not surprisingly, he related to his spouse in a very detached, businesslike manner. Before he can be free to create a deeply connected, celebratory friendship with his spouse, he will first have to see that God relates to him in more than businesslike ways.

Part of caring for a person like that is to find a million ways to say, "God is not like what you've been taught," but you also need to show positively who God is. What better way to do that than to show how the "Rule-Giver" commanded his people to celebrate regularly in a way that showed the party in his heart. This next passage comes early in the Bible, out of writings known collectively as the books of the Law. This is a passage about how to celebrate the good gifts your God has given you with other people:

> You shall tithe all the yield of your seed that comes from the field year by year. And before the LORD your God, in the place that he will choose, to make his name dwell there, you shall eat the tithe of your grain, of your wine, and of your oil, and the firstborn of your herd and flock, that you may learn to fear the LORD your God always. And if the way is too long for you, so that you are not able to carry the tithe, when the LORD your God blesses you, because the place is too far from you, which the LORD your God chooses, to set his name there, then you shall turn it into money and bind up the money in your hand and go to the place that the LORD your God chooses and spend the money for whatever you desire—oxen or sheep or wine or strong drink, whatever your appetite craves. And you shall

eat there before the LORD your God and rejoice, you and your household. And you shall not neglect the Levite who is within your towns, for he has no portion or inheritance with you.

At the end of every three years you shall bring out all the tithe of your produce in the same year and lay it up within your towns. And the Levite, because he has no portion or inheritance with you, and the sojourner, the fatherless, and the widow, who are within your towns, shall come and eat and be filled, that the LORD your God may bless you in all the work of your hands that you do. (Deuteronomy 14:22–29)

Celebrate Lavishly

First, this passage says that you are to total up all the produce your fields have produced, which is another way of saying all the good things God has given to you. You then take a tithe of it—normally understood as 10 percent of the total—and do what with it? Convert it to money so you can carry it, journey to the place where God's presence is, and use the money to buy other food for yourself.

Notice carefully what you are to buy—whatever you desire. That's a pretty broad category. My desires can run pretty high. Are you sure he meant *whatever* I desire?

Well, he clarifies that with several examples. Oxen or sheep—the makings of a good party. Wine—definitely moving in a positive direction. Or if that won't suffice, strong drink. This is starting to sound like a pretty liberal, fun-loving God. Are you getting the point about how lavish he is and how abundant? If you missed it, he adds a further qualification so there's no question of you misreading his heart: *whatever* your appetite craves.

This is not a God who holds good stuff back from you. He is not stoic or restrictive. He is not a killjoy. Rather, he invites you to enjoy yourself. Actually, to be faithful to what he says, he *commands* you to enjoy yourself. This is not an option. You don't get to sit home and decide, "Do I want to go spend money this year on an annual feast? Do I really want to go and enjoy eating whatever my appetite craves?" You don't get a choice. You are commanded to go.

Nor do you get a choice regarding how much you get to spend. When was the last time you took 10 percent of your entire annual income and spent it all on one vacation? Even if you came close a couple of times, I'd wager that it's not every year. Yes, the Israelites were commanded to go and throw a feast every year, using a full tithe of all they made that year.

Welcome to the kingdom of the happy God!

Now, think about your friends. How have you reflected this openhearted lavishness to them? What would it mean to them if you did? How would they respond? How would your lavishness build their confidence that you deeply value them?

I was invited once to a fifty-guest, catered party given by a husband for his wife's special birthday. It was no surprise to hear later that she felt very affirmed by him. He celebrated her lavishly. Does that mean you can celebrate like God does only if you can afford a big party? No. Lavish celebration comes first from your heart that desires to value your relationships. It comes secondarily from your wallet.

One of my prized Christmas decorations came from a couple I counseled *pro bono*. It's a painted wine bottle filled with small Christmas tree lights that the wife made for me. On the same day they gave it to me they told a story of how they were covering their daughter's ten-dollar party tray contribution to the family gathering because she couldn't afford it otherwise. In reality, neither could they. That night I took their gift home and carefully set in on a prominent shelf in our living room because I knew that in their circumstances it was a lavish present. Their celebration of our friendship tells me how deeply they value me.

Celebrate as Part of Worship

Second, make sure that when you feast, you remember it really involves God's kingdom. You are commanded to come and eat before him. This is not a party you throw for yourself in your backyard. You hold it in his presence. That keeps you from pretending that the produce from your fields this year was the result of luck, good fortune, or hard work alone. Rather, you remember that the produce was directly connected to God's sovereign provision for you and your family.

You respond by celebrating the goodness he's brought into your life. You celebrate, keeping your primary benefactor in mind. That's where the balance keeps this from becoming an out of control party. It doesn't become a mind-numbing orgy of gluttony where you eat until you can hardly stand up or think clearly, because it's a celebration of his work on your behalf. It's a reminder that he has gifted you with everything you have and enjoy. Therefore, it's fitting for you to rejoice in his presence.

Take a moment and think about where you have seen God at work in your life to bless you—and not just with physical things. Have you been careful to share with your friends your conviction that the goodness in your life comes from him? Yes, you need to be careful not to brag about what you have, but isn't the opposite (not recognizing his goodness) just as sinful?

What would it look like for you to keep this vertical dimension in view when rejoicing with your friends in the good things God has given you? A couple thoughts come quickly to my mind. Perhaps you do this by sharing publicly at a Thanksgiving service, or maybe you pause during your own Thanksgiving celebration to publicly give God credit for the good things you enjoy.

Let's think even more broadly than that. We don't journey to *a* place *once* a year to celebrate God's goodness. Now that Christ has come, we celebrate twenty-four hours a day, seven days a week. Simple things like saying grace before a meal don't have to be merely habit. It can be heartfelt rejoicing in God's presence for what he's given.

Or consider making time once a week to reflect on God's gifts and invite a close friend to rejoice with you. Drumming a steady beat of gratitude and recognition of what God *has* done for you will keep you from damaging your friendships by wondering what they can do for you.

Celebrate with Others

Third, it's fitting that you not celebrate by yourself. Nor is it enough to merely surround yourself with family and relatives. Instead, you open this celebration to more people, specifically to those who are unable to hold their own celebrations.

You look for ways to invite others to rejoice with you as you rejoice. In the Old Testament, they didn't neglect the Levite. That was important because the Levite didn't have the benefit of lands to produce wealth for him or his family. They did not inherit land because the Lord was their inheritance, but that didn't mean they were to be shortchanged on this earth.

The same was true of the sojourner (the alien), orphans, and widows. Those groups of people were typically identified because they had the least access to the resources of the community and were not likely to enjoy the good gifts that God gave throughout the land. Part of loving each other involves including each other in our rejoicing.

It is so easy for me to drift back to believing that I am the center of gravity for all my relationships, including the vertical one I have with God. Nothing quashes rejoicing like that misbelief. If you want to push against that drift, you need to actively share God's goodness with others, especially those who can't repay you. One

Christmas, instead of giving presents we didn't need, my sister led us to celebrate the season by donating to an overseas organization that cared for needy children. And I felt cheated.

Do you know how good it was for me to wrestle with my greediness and realize one more time how I think *the* measure of relationships is how much I get out of them? That year she and her husband helped us all continue to learn that the goodness God pours into our lives isn't simply for us to enjoy. It's to be shared.

That more openhearted rejoicing attitude affects people. It either invites them to expand their hearts as they join you in sharing all they have or it repulses them, revealing how self-centered their relational commitment is. My underlying selfishness in relationships became really clear when I was unable to rejoice deep in my heart over the benefits those children received. I am glad that experience helped me learn better to genuinely rejoice when others are blessed.

> We learn to celebrate the good things God brings into our own lives and the goodness he gives to others. We do so because we see beyond the things themselves to the Giver of all good things.

You have been brought into a family that rejoices together. We learn to celebrate the good things God brings into our own lives and the goodness he gives to others. We do so because we see beyond the things themselves to the Giver of all good things. So we can rejoice in a world where suffering, sickness, and pain are evident because they are not the last word. Our gift-giving God has entered our dark world and continues to pour out his goodness in ways that point us back to himself.

When you invite others to experience the things this God has given you, you're giving them an even greater invitation to know a God who is this good. When you accept those invitations from others to rejoice in the good things they have, you show how deeply satisfied you are with this God. You are truly happy that you and your friend have felt his touch in your lives. It's a necessary part of loving one another.

On Your Own

1. List as many gifts as you can think of that God has showered on you over the past three months. If you have trouble remembering them, ask your close friends to help you see them more clearly. Take a moment to thank the Lord and reflect on his goodness to you. How do his gifts point you to himself as the bigger, better gift?

2. When was the last time you repented over coveting, envying, and being jealous? Whose faces quickly come to mind when you think about wanting what others have? Ask Jesus to help you see that he's already given you something of much greater worth than all the things you long for—himself. Ask him to help you see his beauty, greatness, worth, and value so you can cherish him that much more.

3. Does your style of rejoicing match the greatness of your rescuing, redeeming, gift-giving God? Is it abundant, overflowing, and full of life? Or do you tend toward stinginess, restraint, and minimalism? What does your rejoicing—or lack thereof—say about the value you place on him?

4. Take the next twenty-four hours to look hard for good things happening to people around you and enter into their joy with them. Smile when you see them. Let them know you're happy for them. Look for ways to share with them how their good fortune helps you see Jesus more clearly.

CHAPTER 14

Peaceful Love: Living Harmoniously with Each Other

In the garden of Eden, there was peace. Peace with God, between people and with the rest of the creatures. Then Satan introduced his own special creation that he had earlier taken to heaven: strife. That was not a relational trait he learned from his Creator, but was his own adaptation—an adaptation we humans fully embraced.

Since then, relationships have never been the same. It doesn't matter whether you look at relationships from a national level or down at the individual, you live in a world far more marked by war-making than by peaceful coexistence.

But God refused to leave us locked in strife. He could've fought fire with fire, ending our antagonism by crushing us. But he didn't. Rather, he reintroduced peace into relationships by reconciling us to himself (2 Corinthians 5:19). That same peacemaking impulse that drives him spills over into our lives so that we long to live peacefully with each other.

There is no longer strife in heaven, and the time is coming when there won't be any on earth either. But we don't have to wait until then. This chapter looks at how peaceful love allows us now to enjoy the goodness of relationships that grow closer despite our differences. More than that, when we love this way we proclaim a surprising God, one who successfully brings peace to this present world as we anticipate the next.

Human Solutions for War Don't Produce True Peace

Throughout history there are two primary modes of dealing with antagonism in relationships, both of which regularly miss their intended goal: either forcibly impose peace or give in to someone's demands.

The formation of the country of Yugoslavia was an attempt to compel peace through force. After World War II its Communist government—backed by a strong, unified military—bound together several diverse cultural factions in the region to create what looked like one nation. The fiction of that peaceful coexistence became clear in the 1990s, however, as that "one nation" violently broke into the independent countries of Bosnia and Herzegovina, Croatia, Kosovo, Macedonia, Montenegro, Serbia, and Slovenia. When a single country spontaneously divides into eight, you realize there wasn't much real peace among the factions to begin with. There may have been an absence of hostilities, but that doesn't mean there was the presence of peace.

And that only makes sense. Using force to coerce peace is a strategy that relies on war, so how could it produce true peace? There are times when it is appropriate to use force to control enemies and curb hostilities, but, in and of itself, force is a warlike tactic that cannot eliminate war.

Anyone who has relied on force or threat as part of his parenting strategy knows only too well how it doesn't produce deeply connected relationships where people move toward each other. Instead it creates scenarios where the children either rebel as they assert their own personalities or become wretchedly subservient, losing their personality. Neither outcome fosters a strong mutual connection. The result is the same for spouses and friends when elements of war play a significant role in the relationship.

A second approach our world uses to create peace is trying to appease an antagonist. The hope is that you can win over the hearts of others when you "Wage Peace, Not War." It's a catchy slogan, but its proponents often don't take into account the nature of people who are determined to misuse power. Appeasing a bully never brings peace—it merely buys you time until he or she demands something else from you.

Again, this is easy to see on the world stage. Neville Chamberlain, Britain's Prime Minister before the Second World War, learned the hard way that appeasement is an unstable strategy when he flew to Germany in the fall of 1938. He attempted to win peace by giving Adolf Hitler part of Czechoslovakia. After returning to England, he stood outside his office before the crowd assembled there and read from the new agreement:

> My good friends, this is the second time in our history that there has come back from Germany to Downing Street peace with honour. I believe it is peace for our time. We thank you from the bottom of our hearts. And now I recommend you to go home and sleep quietly in your beds.[1]

Germany demonstrated the failure of his policy when they invaded the rest of Czechoslovakia only half a year later and plunged the world into its second global war. Chamberlain was as ineffective at leading his country into peace as he had been in predicting its arrival. Promising peace is easy; producing it is much harder.

What takes place on the world stage is a magnification of what happens on a smaller, individual scale. Have you ever watched a parent attempt to bribe her child? "If you behave in the store/church/Grandpa's house then you'll get a candy bar/stuffed animal/movie." This is a strategy that can only lead to frustration, never to mutual respect.

To remain effective, the bribe has to increase to keep pace with the child's developing wants and desires, often exhausting the parent's creativity and resources. In addition, the child is not acting in order to form deep attachments to his parent, but to enrich himself. It's a strategy that fosters relational war by reinforcing the child's innate selfishness.

The same dynamic takes place in adult relationships. Once you begin down the road of appeasement with an abusive husband or belligerent neighbor, it takes an ever-increasing amount to keep the other person happy, none of which ever brings harmony to your relationship.

Living peacefully with each other is just as hard for Christians as it is for anyone else. If you've followed Christ for more than a few months, you know how easily we war with each other. We fight over which doctrines are true, the right way to live them out, how much water to use in baptism (including when to use it and which procedure), which candidate to vote for, the best way to school our children, which movie ratings are okay, what color the sanctuary carpet should be . . . and the list goes on.

Not only do we strongly disagree over many things, we resolve our disagreements badly. You probably know more than a few people who have chosen to leave a church over such a disagreement. "Oh, I just can't go *there* anymore. You should hear what they did." War comes easily to us.

We War with Each Other Because We War with God

Any external solution to the problem of relational warring ultimately proves ineffective in producing peace because it doesn't deal with the source of our war-making impulse. Without a change at that internal level, longings for peace start to feel hopeless, like a sentimental Christmas card that cannot produce what it proclaims. "May you have peace this time of year . . . if people decide to be nice to you . . . if your parents get off your back . . . if no one complains about their present . . . if the car doesn't need repairs . . . if a tree doesn't fall on your house . . . if the planets align properly . . . if . . ."

Jimi Hendrix showed great insight when he said, "When the power of love overcomes the love of power, the world will know peace."[2]

It's great poetry and probably true. But it's not very likely to happen because it misses the reality that the love of power is not easily removed. It ignores the strength of the nature of fallen humanity.

So did the Dalai Lama when he said, "Of course, the mind could rationalize fighting back, but the heart would never understand. Then you would be divided in yourself: the heart and the mind, and the war would be inside of you."[3]

He gives a beautiful description of the insanity of war, but misses that we are already at war, that war lodges deep within our humanity. Part of our nature when we're born is that we are at war with our Maker. That war spills over so that we fight with everyone around us, including those who are closest to us.

No one has to teach you to live at war. I still remember the moment my beautiful three-week-old daughter screamed in my face when she understood I was not going to give her what she wanted. She didn't rest quietly in peaceful confidence that I would meet her needs. Instead she used the limited means at her disposal to make sure I knew that she and I were not okay in that moment. All this without the ability to put logical thoughts together. The war comes early. Precognitive, preverbal, but clearly at war.

What parent has not experienced a slippery, squirmy little person bent on having his or her own way, even if that came at the expense of the person who loved and cared for him or her? A young couple told me about their one-and-a-half-year-old son who arches his back on airplanes to make it impossible to hold him. He also doesn't believe that they're doing what is best for him so he literally throws everything he has against their desires.

This internal war starts at birth and simply gets more subtle and creative as we age. Children who are gifted in war-making grow up to be gifted adults. According to Romans 1:18–32, our inability to live peacefully with each other is an outflow of a deeper problem: we war with each other because we war with God.

Jesus Ends the War by Making Peace

Thankfully, God doesn't respond to your antagonism toward him with threats or bribery. War-making is not his first response to rebellion. If it were, you would never have peace with him, which means you would remain at war with others, including those closest to you. Instead he works to forge peace.

Sitting at his last Passover meal, just before he went to offer his life for his friends, Jesus said to his disciples, "Peace I leave with you; my peace I give to you. Not as the world gives do I give to you. Let not your hearts be troubled, neither let them be afraid" (John 14:27). He understood that offering peace is a big promise to hold out because it is hard to actually produce. Yet he was bold because he knew how he intended to bring it about.

He didn't simply hold out peace as a nice hope. He gave it in the moment, then he left to free them from the war that bound their hearts so they could enjoy true peace. Not the simple absence of war, but the presence of a positive relationship—one in which they were reconciled to the one they had hated. This way they would no longer desire war, but crave his friendship.

The proof that Jesus was able to resolve the war they had started with their Maker is in what he said to them when he returned from the dead. He greeted his people repeatedly by saying, "Peace be with you" (John 20:19, 21, 26). His peace is not as the world gives. He went to hell and back in order to bring peace—not simply to offer it as a nice wish, but as a solid reality. He proved, once and for all that he truly was the Prince of Peace who was prophesied to come ages earlier (Isaiah 9:6).

There is no more wrath and anger from your Maker once you've been reconciled to him. He dealt with the internal problem so that your heart could no longer be troubled. Now that you have peace with him, the two of you will never be at war again. Even your present failures do not rekindle war in your heart nor judgment in his. That's the glory of Jesus' peace. Real peace does not leave you, not even when you sin. Instead, it continues growing, pulling you toward him like an irresistible magnet.

The same happens with your human friendships as you love them by offering to live peacefully with others.

We Live in Peace

Weak, immature love insists that we can be peaceful only when we have complete agreement with each other. More mature love has learned how to agree to disagree because it knows that disagreeing doesn't have to divide. Paul gets at this idea in his letter to the Philippians:

> Let those of us who are mature think this way [along the lines of what he's been saying], and if in anything you think otherwise, God will reveal that also to you. Only let us hold true to what we have attained. (Philippians 3:15–16)

The apostle Paul understood that not everyone agreed with him. More than that, he made room for their disagreement. That's not an excuse for compromise. He was not afraid to rebuke people when their beliefs challenged the essentials of a life wrapped up in Jesus (for example, Galatians 1:6–9). But Paul made room for working things out without breaking relationships. He knew that there is room for living together with our differences.

Have you ever stopped to think how one additional verse in the Bible would have clarified so many of the differences between Christians? All God would have had to do to end hundreds of years of disagreements among millions of believers was add one verse that said: "Christian baptism is/is not for infants" or "believers will/will not live through the final tribulation." One verse would have been enough to end all debate.

Why didn't he? My former colleague David Powlison hit the nail squarely on the head when he suggested that part of God's purpose is to teach us that love must transcend our disagreements. Only by living peacefully with people whom we disagree with can some facets of real love be seen. Only then are those facets necessary.

> ... part of God's purpose is to teach us that love must transcend our disagreements. Only by living peacefully with people whom we disagree with can some facets of real love be seen.

You can see that reality in my politically integrated neighborhood. I live next door to an ardent Democrat on one side and an equally ardent Republican on another. To balance everyone, an ardent Libertarian lives across the street. If you want to live in my neighborhood, you're going to have to talk politics at some point.

Now, I don't fully agree with any of them, but we're friends because our friendship is deeper than our political leanings. We work on each other's houses and yards. Several times a year we all get together for a neighborhood party. And the guys throw horseshoes together one night a week throughout the summer. Our political differences don't destroy our neighborhood. We can live at peace. Peacefulness doesn't mean mealy-mouthed compromise, nor does it mean 100 percent agreement.

Is that hard for you? I think it is for many of us. You may have grown up in a world where disagreement wasn't allowed regardless of whether it was your politics or personality. Where a difference of opinion or belief was so strongly challenged that you learned not to hold an alternative. Or where others regularly tried to change your mind by constantly questioning your thoughts or preferences. Or maybe the only option you had was to withdraw into yourself.

If that was the case, how are you making space for people to disagree with you without putting your relationship at risk? Living peacefully is often most difficult when we're talking about the people we spend the most time with. Is your spouse allowed to have a different taste in music while you're in the room? Can your girlfriend hold a deep conviction that her kids need to be in the public school while you homeschool yours? Can you support a child who is finding an authentic connection with Christ in a tradition other than the one that speaks deeply to you? Are your son's piercings and tattoos really worth destroying your relationship over? Are your daughter's? Where is it a struggle for you to respect and support your closest relationships?

In the list of the fruit of the Spirit, there are no conditions put on other people. God doesn't say you are to be kind when others are kind, or that you need to be tender only to those who treat you tenderly, or that you should forgive only those who are easy to forgive. Instead, as with all the fruit of the Spirit, peace is most needed when people are most difficult—when they rub you the wrong way. And thankfully, because it is the result of the Spirit living in you, you can respond peacefully even when other people are not at their best.

The Prince of Peace redeems people who learn how to live in peace.

We Long for Peace

A peace-living community comes from a peace-longing community. One age-old way that humanity has attempted to make peace is by burying the hatchet—in each other's heads. Retaliation—forcing someone to feel what he caused you to feel—is as common as it is ineffective. All that does is create a cycle of retribution, as witnessed by the blood feuds around the world that span generations.

Most students of history realize quickly that no one race has a monopoly on being victimized by another race. In fact, you would be hard-pressed to find one race that hasn't been oppressed at some point in its history. And those victimizations often generate retaliatory movements that can last for hundreds of years.

A peace-longing community approaches the problem of wrongs committed in a different way. In Mark's Gospel, we're told about a praying person who does not interact with a person who has sinned against him. Jesus counsels him, "And whenever you stand praying, forgive, if you have anything against anyone, so that your Father also who is in heaven may forgive you your trespasses" (Mark 11:25).

A wrong has been done. We're not told how severe it is. It could be something small, but if it comes to your mind in the middle of praying, I would guess it's probably on the weightier side. The size, however, is irrelevant to the point Jesus makes. What is important is that someone has wronged you and the memory of it pushes itself forward and gets in the way of your prayers.

Notice that the other person is not physically present. It's just you and God. And Jesus tells you to forgive him before you do anything else. In other words, forgiveness can take place without the other person being present. That's not the same as saying, "It's all good now between us." But it is hopeful.

Some people who have sinned against you are not physically available. You've moved or they've moved so you couldn't find them if you wanted to. Perhaps they've even died. But you don't need them to be physically present because you don't need their permission to forgive them. All you need is the desire to live in peace with others.

The internal attitude that expresses itself in forgiveness sets the foundation for any interaction that might take place in the future between you and the other person. It happens in your heart. It is a free letting go of the debt so that, as far as you are concerned, it is now canceled and you are no longer trying to wring it from the other person.

Is there someone who comes to mind whom you're holding something against? Could you consider letting go of the bitterness that threatens to engulf you? What if it's an ungrateful child who's stolen from you? A two-faced friend who badmouths you to others? An abusive parent who never apologized? A spouse who on his own repeatedly alters the decisions you've made together? You can think about letting go only if you long for peace like Jesus longs for peace. That happens only as you reexperience the wonder of him canceling your debt.

If you struggle to let go, do three things: (1) take some time to remind yourself of all that Jesus has forgiven you, (2) add to your list by asking him to forgive you this one more time for preferring to keep the war going in your heart after all he's not held against you, and then (3) ask him to replace your bitterness with a longing to live in peace.

We Restore Peace

A peace-living, peace-longing community is also a peace-reconciling community. It is a community that learns how to hear each other's grievances, to clarify the differences where appropriate, and to ask for forgiveness for things that were wrong. Jesus tells us to be reconciled with others.

> "So if you are offering your gift at the altar and there remember that your brother has something against you, leave your gift there before the altar and go. First be reconciled to your brother, and then come and offer your gift." (Matthew 5:23–24)

When you realize you've wronged someone, even if—maybe *especially* if—you're worshipping when you realize it, you need to stop what you're doing and go make things right with your brother.

There have been a number of times when Sally and I have not had a good Sunday morning, and I've been the primary antagonist. We walk into church after having made war that morning, and I am just stuck in my self-righteousness about how she started it or how right I was, and so on. During the service I've felt the Lord's conviction and the subsequent need to apologize. I've had to lean over then and ask her to forgive me for the ways I sinned against her. If you live in this community of peace, you will learn to think about how other people might be offended by what you've done. And you act to make things right.

Later in Matthew, Jesus' command is slightly different: "If your brother sins against you, go and tell him his fault, between you and him alone. If he listens to you, you have gained your brother" (Matthew 18:15). Again, you are to go to the other person, but this time the fault is hers, not yours.

Notice how active Jesus intends for you to be in reconciling relationships. Whether you've caused the problem or been on the receiving end of it, you are to actively restore peace between the two of you. You are to work to fix the relationship—to regain your brother.

This does not always mean that you and the other person are in perfect harmony again. Sometimes, even when you've sorted through all the problems between the two of you, you still need to go through the process of reestablishing trust, which takes time. The point of pursuing one another for reconciliation is to lay the groundwork that would lead to the possibility of being close friends and partners again.

In Acts 15, we're told that Paul and Barnabas completed their first missionary journey by traveling to Jerusalem. There, they participated in the first church council. This gathering worked to establish greater unity and peace within the early church. After this victory for peace, Paul and Barnabas had such a sharp disagreement that they went their separate ways.

> And after some days Paul said to Barnabas, "Let us return and visit the brothers in every city where we proclaimed the word of the Lord, and see how they are." Now Barnabas wanted to take with them John called Mark. But Paul thought best not to take with them one who had withdrawn from them in Pamphylia and had not gone with them to the work. And there arose a sharp disagreement, so that they separated from each other. Barnabas took Mark with him and sailed away to Cyprus, but Paul chose Silas and departed, having been commended by the brothers to the grace of the Lord. And he went through Syria and Cilicia, strengthening the churches. (Acts 15:36–41)

These were not young, immature believers. They were seasoned veterans, filled with the Holy Spirit. Yet they held opposite beliefs regarding the idea of bringing John Mark along. Those beliefs were so strong that they broke apart this team, a team that had functioned so well together that we never had a hint of a problem. But look at 2 Timothy 4:11, where Paul says, "Luke alone is with me. Get Mark and bring him with you, for he is very useful to me for ministry."

You don't see the process of reconciliation, but you do see the results. There is peace among the family. Did Paul reach out? Did Mark? It doesn't matter. What matters is that the desire for peace was so strong that one or both of them couldn't let the matter rest until it was resolved. When it was resolved they were able to again be partners in building the kingdom, despite Paul's earlier misgivings. A community of peace knows how to pursue reconciliation.

The length of time it takes to bring peace is less important than the direction you are moving in your relationships. One courageous family I know had deep relational disconnects at every level, but they wanted something better. So they began to talk—siblings to each other, children to their parents, parents to each other, and parents to the children. Those conversations over years led to more discussions among them that fostered even greater desires to reconnect. Though they are still in process and will be until they stand in heaven (just like the rest of us), they are being drawn together, experiencing greater peace than they had before.

If you're human, you probably have some outstanding broken relationships. When was the last time you felt a longing to restore one of them? Don't push aside those indications of love when they come. See them as signals that it's time to pursue peace with that person again.

We Don't Disrupt Peace

Finally, although it may sound counterintuitive, the community of peace also knows how to leave people alone. Jesus emphasizes that we must pursue peace and reconciliation, but what do you do if the other person does not want peace? How do you pursue someone who resists you? You don't.

Lynn was upset. Over the years her adult daughter had

increasingly isolated herself from all family members and friends. She restricted all communication and cut people off if they didn't agree with her perspective. Lynn had been able to maintain a connection with her, but it was always tenuous at best. She asked me, "How can I have a relationship with my daughter? What else do I need to do?"

My heart went out to her because, from what I could tell, she really had gone the second, third, and probably seventeenth mile with her daughter. So I pulled my Bible off the shelf and turned with her to Romans 12:18 where we read together, "If possible, so far as it depends on you, live peaceably with all." You have the responsibility, as much as you possibly can, to live peacefully with everyone. That's a weighty responsibility that you have to take seriously. And yet, isn't it wonderful that Paul starts that sentence with "If"? If possible. He acknowledges that it is not always possible.

Some people just don't want to live in peace. They are set on living the way they want to, and they don't care about the effect that has on anyone else. They make it impossible to live peacefully because of the conditions they set on having a relationship with them.

It is not your job to contort yourself around all of their conditions to have "peace." Nor do you swing the pendulum to the opposite extreme and continue banging on a closed door, demanding that they come out and engage the larger world around them. You don't hound them or badger them. You leave them be. In other words, you decide to live peacefully with them by not creating a situation that invites or provokes war.

We Rely on Jesus to Bring Peace

You pursue a peaceful lifestyle because peace is more important to God than it has ever been to you. When you get tired of trying to reconcile with broken sinners, remind yourself that you have not yet given up all of your rights and privileges, including your own life, in order to make peace happen. Jesus has. And now he gives his peace to you as he invites you to carry on the work he started—building peaceful relationships.

> *When you get tired of trying to reconcile with broken sinners, remind yourself that you have not yet given up all of your rights and privileges, including your own life, in order to make peace happen.*

On Your Own

1. When was the last time you meditated on the peace Jesus has brought between you and himself—on how much you needed it and how little you could do to produce it? Take a moment and let him know how much you appreciate what he has done.

2. There is little that shows how deeply you've grasped the essence of the gospel like your own desire to live at peace with God and others. Think for a moment about what most characterizes your relationships—peace, war, or mere tolerance?

3. What are the broken relationships in your life? Have you been able to sort out the pieces that you contributed? When was the last time you prayed for them or for reconciliation?

4. Is this a time for going to those people or for realizing that they have made it not possible at this time? Who has God given you in your life—friend, neighbor, small group leader, pastor—to help you sort out that answer?

CHAPTER 15

Hospitable Love: Showing Kindness without Grumbling

The last aspect of loving well that we'll explore is hospitable love. There are times when loving others as Jesus loves us means we choose to let their needs break into our lives, disrupting our schedules and comforts. We honor them by deciding that their need trumps whatever else we had planned, even if they can never pay us back. Being *generously interruptible* is a necessary component of your relationships that comes from the heart of how Christ relates to you.

Jesus doesn't make you wait with your need until a preset time that he has made available to you. Instead, he invites you to bring your needs to him as they arise. And you are willing to do so because you know that he really wants to hear from you and help you in that moment because he loves you. His love is not locked within tightly controlled parameters.

When you are hospitable to others, you reflect God's way of relating to you. This aspect of love emphasizes that caring relationships will offer you the chance to lose control of your schedule. Your loss, however, results in a much deeper connection with someone in real need. Hospitality can be hard on you, but it communicates even more powerfully how much you value someone else.

Hospitality Is Messy and Inconvenient

I don't like being interrupted by someone else's need. I remember how annoyed I was one Saturday morning when I went downstairs to answer the door and Renée asked, "Can I get my check?" The day before had been payday at the ministry where I served as business manager, but Renée hadn't shown up for work. I grumbled as I went back upstairs to get the keys to my office across the street. I threw a gruff, "I have to go pay someone," over my shoulder to Sally as I trudged back downstairs.

Multiple scenarios ran through my head about what kept Renée out of work that day, but not one of my guesses even tried to give her the benefit of the doubt. I didn't want to think well of her. No doubt she needed the money that morning to take care of things that couldn't wait, but I didn't care. I didn't want to be in that building on my day off, and I certainly didn't want my home life disturbed.

Even though I was involved in ministry at the time, I wasn't very good at love. I held onto a nine-to-five mentality. During work hours, I was willing to give up lots of my own comfort for the sake of others. That was my job. But once I went home, I considered myself off the clock and therefore no longer available for someone else's needs or disruptions. Renée broke into my carefully prescribed boundaries and made me realize that what I thought of as love was rather anemic.

Those few moments on a Saturday morning were nothing compared to the interruptions I experienced moving people into where I lived. For several years I shared a house with two guys who had worked as counselors in an addiction recovery program. They understood how difficult it was to transition from a program back into mainstream life, and they cared deeply about the people they had worked with. So several times we moved someone in who needed a place to stay for a few months while he got on his feet again.

Each time we did, it required an adjustment from everyone. The new guy had to get used to our household, and we had to get used to him—his personality, work requirements, social connections, habits, eccentricities, and quirks. Hospitality is messy. It's inconvenient and disruptive. And my heart cries against it.

> *Hospitality requires me to invite people to invade the fragile cocoon of predictability I attempt to build.*

I like having a smooth-running life. Hospitality requires me to invite people to invade the fragile cocoon of predictability I attempt to build. That's hard, because all bets are off as to how they'll affect my world. I don't like that.

What's that like for you? How well do you respond when your friend drops by to say:

- "Hey, if the electric lines break from all the snow and you still have power, can we camp out with you?"
- "Can I borrow half a dozen eggs and some sugar for the cake I'm making tonight?"
- "My girlfriend is coming out to visit, and I was wondering if she could stay with you so that we can avoid temptation or the appearance that we're sleeping together?"
- "My #@%&*! brother just poked his nose into my family's business and I'm ready to put a hole through the wall. Do you have a few minutes to help me sort this out?"

Do you gladly welcome the intrusion and demand on your resources, or do you struggle?

Learning from an Old Master

If you're like me, your bad attitudes toward hospitality need to be replaced by those that more accurately reflect God's concerns for people in need. I'm challenged by what I see from Abraham's response to three strangers who, unannounced, pulled up alongside his tent in the wilderness.

> And the LORD appeared to him [Abraham] by the oaks of Mamre, as he sat at the door of his tent in the heat of the day. He lifted up his eyes and looked, and behold, three men were standing in front of him. When he saw them, he ran from the tent door to meet them and bowed himself to the earth and said, "O Lord, if I have found favor in your sight, do not pass by your servant. Let a little water be brought, and wash your feet, and rest yourselves under the tree, while I bring a morsel of bread, that you may refresh yourselves, and after that you may pass on—since you have come to your servant." So they said, "Do as you have said." And Abraham went quickly into the tent to Sarah and said, "Quick! Three seahs of fine flour! Knead it, and make cakes." And Abraham ran to the herd and took a calf, tender and good, and gave it to a young man, who prepared it quickly. Then he took curds and milk and the calf that he had prepared, and set it before them. And he stood by them under the tree while they ate. (Genesis 18:1–8)

It would be easy to safely tuck this story away under the heading of Ancient Middle Eastern Culture (which is about the same as the heading, "Nothing to Do with Me"). The author of Hebrews 13:2, however, found things to learn from Abraham thousands of years later when he urged, "Do not neglect to show hospitality to strangers, for thereby some have entertained angels unawares." Clearly this verse refers back to Abraham as he waited on his visitors, not knowing at first who they were.

I suspect there are at least three important attitudes you and I can pick up from this encounter as well.

Watch for Opportunities to Be Hospitable

Notice first that Abraham hurries to meet the strangers when he sees them. Think about that. It's the heat of the day. You're sleepily sitting in the door of your tent, maybe dozing on and off. Just taking it easy. And then these three interruptions are standing there. Caring for them means giving away some of your resources. Worse, you're going to have to put out a lot of work and energy during the most uncomfortable time of the day.

Wouldn't it be easier to pretend that you hadn't seen them? Sort of like that stranded motorist you cruise by on the highway, keeping your foot steady on the gas and your eyes locked on the bumper in front of you. Abraham could just stay there—maybe even let his eyes drift closed so it would be true that he didn't see them. He could rationalize that travelers surely would be smart enough to carry enough provisions for the trip. "No one sets out on a journey through the wilderness without making sure they've got enough to get there, right? They'll be fine."

Abraham doesn't do that. He's not standoffish, waiting for them to come to him. Instead, he gets up and hurries to meet them. He's ninety-nine years old, running in the heat of the desert day . . . for what? Is he afraid someone else will get to them first? That they might leave if he doesn't? You learn something about hospitality by watching him. Hospitality involves you quickly going out, looking for needs to meet.

Abraham illustrates what God means when he commands us to "seek to show hospitality" (Romans 12:13). The verb has an aspect of looking for opportunities, not waiting for them to show up, but proactively finding them. In order to show hospitality, you need to have your eyes open and your mind alert to the needs around you.

Did you pay attention to how Abraham meets the needs he sees? I always smile at the irony of his saying "Quick!" followed by what he tells Sarah to do: "Quick! Three seahs of fine flour! Knead it, and make cakes." Making that much bread would be anything but quick, even if Sarah weren't nearly one hundred years old. Modern equivalents are always hard to nail down, but our best understanding is that he told her to grab the equivalent of twenty quarts of flour. If my bread machine uses one-and-one-half to two cups of flour per loaf, he's just told her to make at least forty loaves of bread . . . quick!

Notice too that they're not using coarse flour, but the fine stuff that would have been more costly. Nothing too good for the guests. And as if that weren't enough, he has a calf from his herd prepared for them—and the implication is that it's all for them, as he stands watching them eat. His is a generous response to people he doesn't know who have dropped by unannounced.

Again, as I've invited you throughout this book, start with yourself. What kind of attitude do you have regarding the needs of others? Do you share my tightly scripted nine-to-five mindset or do you have a greater longing to notice and respond generously, even if that's inconvenient for you?

Think about the people around you. Are you quickly aware of what they need or do you have to have special announcements to get your attention?

You're Called to Care for the Needy

Second, notice how Abraham recognizes that this is a God-ordained moment. He didn't engage in a long, drawn-out, soul-searching session with the Lord. "Oh, God, is this an interruption that you're bringing me? Is this part of what you want me to do with my day?" He assumed that if these guys were in his section of the wilderness, then by definition, it was his God-given responsibility to be hospitable. He didn't sit there, believing that it was someone else's job to take care of them.

The broad development of the welfare state over the past century makes it very easy to believe that the responsibility for helping people in need lies primarily with the government. Now, it is a great thing if you live in a country where the larger social structure tries to provide for the poor, the needy, and the disadvantaged. *But* that is not a mission God has given to the government. He has given that job to his church.

When Paul discussed his ministry to the Gentiles with the leaders of the church in Jerusalem, everything he was doing sounded great to them. "Only, they asked us to remember the poor, the very thing I was eager to do" (Galatians 2:10). The church is called to care for the poor. If others want to be involved too, that's great. But we must never allow their involvement to help us forget that first and foremost, it's the calling and the privilege of the church to care for the poor.

I forget that so easily. One of the early responses our church took to the economic crisis that began in 2008 was to start a food pantry for anyone in need. When I first heard of this initiative, my knee-jerk reaction was, "There's too much need. We'll never be able to do it. We'll be swamped and bankrupt. Maybe we could tap into the government-sponsored food bank." Isn't it interesting that my initial thoughts were, "Let's depend on the government to provide for our needs"?

I've since repented. The congregation brought in more food than we were able to give away—and we gave away a lot. People regularly brought donations like we asked—then they went the second mile. On their own initiative, several people approached various stores in the area to ask if they would donate either gift cards or food they would have to throw away. We ended up with so much food we had the joy of contacting other churches to see if they knew anyone whom we could bless. It was a little like watching the loaves and fish multiply.

It has been so good for me to repent. And it's been great to see the church taking on her job of proactively caring for the poor and the needy. Traditionally, we had reached out around Thanksgiving and Christmas, but we've now had the privilege of learning that since the need does not exist only at certain times of the year, the impulse to generosity cannot exist only then either.

Bring it closer to home. Is there someone from your small group who's just had an operation or who can't get around well? Have you thought about cooking extra and taking it to her? Or maybe you need to proactively invite someone in. I know one family that welcomed a single person into their home during the time he was recovering from surgery. He couldn't take care of himself and needed help that he wouldn't get living on his own.

Hospitable people actively look for ways to care generously for people around them. This starts with those you're closest to. Take a moment and ask yourself if you've inadvertently overlooked any needs that your friends and neighbors might have.

Expect to Be Inconvenienced

Third, I learn from Abraham that hospitality is rarely convenient. It is not convenient to have strangers drop by. It's not convenient to make bread and prepare a calf. More convenient would be for Abraham to say, "Quick, pull the mold off the old bread that's going bad!" Convenient would be, "Quick, grab some leftovers!" Inconvenient is cooking for half the day and then watching people you barely know eat.

So much of my "hospitality" is conveniently planned. I try to schedule my care of others so I stay in control of whose needs penetrate my barriers. I decide how much energy, time, and resources I will give as well as determining whom I will give to. I like being hospitable to people who can afford to wait or who don't need very much. In other words, I like being hospitable to people who don't need my hospitality.

True hospitality is different. Like strangers at your door in the heat of the day—or on Saturday morning—it never seems to fit into your timetable. Jesus told a parable about a man who needed to borrow food at midnight for a friend who had just shown up at his house (Luke 11:5–8). Not the best moment to have an unexpected need, nor the best time to reach out and ask for some help, nor even a good occasion to be asked. But what a great setting to illustrate the need for desperate, persistent prayers. The people hearing this parable understood that hospitality rarely fits into anyone's well-ordered schedule.

> If you're unwilling to be inconvenienced, you're unwilling to love hospitably.

It certainly didn't for my parents and me the morning we were awakened by someone urgently pounding on our front door. That was not the most convenient time to have our neighbor drop by, but escaping an abusive husband is not something most people plan either. If you're unwilling to be inconvenienced, you're unwilling to love hospitably.

Hospitality Is Based on Need, Not Reciprocity

Are you starting to realize that hospitality is not the same as inviting your friends over to dinner? Hospitality moves well beyond tit-for-tat, where I give you a present because you gave me a present. It goes well beyond Christmas card guilt, where I can hardly imagine anything worse than receiving a card from someone I didn't send one to. It's not the same as hosting a party for friends who could afford to have you to one of their own. Jesus left some detailed instructions about hospitality.

> *...hospitality is not the same as inviting your friends over to dinner*

"When you give a dinner or a banquet, do not invite your friends or your brothers or your relatives or rich neighbors, lest they also invite you in return and you be repaid. But when you give a feast, invite the poor, the crippled, the lame, the blind, and you will be blessed, because they cannot repay you. You will be repaid at the resurrection of the just." (Luke 14:12–14).

Hospitality means giving freely to someone who has less than you, who will be disadvantaged if you don't give, and who will never be able to repay you.

> *Hospitality means giving freely to someone who has less than you, who will be disadvantaged if you don't give, and who will never be able to repay you.*

I can still barely believe Steve's incredible openhearted offer. He and I had been acquaintances at our college fellowship several years earlier, but we'd been out of touch until my wife and I began attending his church. We were getting ready to move to the town where he lived, but we didn't yet have a place to stay nor, since I was a full-time seminary student, did we have much income.

"You could come live with us," Steve said. "We don't have much, but we have an extra bedroom that you're welcome to." That initial conversation carried over into others involving his wife and led to us living with them for the next year in a way that we could never repay. It was a very gracious offer that embodied the spirit of true hospitality worthy of the name *Christian*.

Hospitality Involves Risks

If you had the chance, I can imagine you might say to me, "But if I go down this road, someone might take advantage of me. Hospitality like that is risky!" If that's what you're thinking, you're right. It is risky. The fictional priest in *Les Miserables* discovered just how risky hospitality can be when Jean Valjean not only stole his silver, but assaulted him in the process. As glorious as his response is in pardoning Valjean and acting as God's agent of redemption, I imagine not many people long to imitate him.

It would be very tempting at this point to let yourself think only about generic strangers needing hospitality. If you do that, your mind will tend to conjure up images that are striking but remote. Homeless men sleeping on city steam vents. Jews living in Europe during the Second World War. Those images may stir you, but if such pictures are far from your normal experience, they can just as easily insulate you from noticing the needs of people right around you.

One way to counter that distance is to think about your friends or family and ask, "What does _____ need from me that she could never repay?" A sheltered place to decompress from the office? A few hours of free babysitting so she could be with her husband? An invitation to a cup of coffee in the middle of a trying day? A safe place to pour out her story of what her family's been going through during the past few months? Where do you need to lay down your schedule for someone else in a way that they could not do the same for you?

Ironically, those smaller, simpler examples are just as loving as the ones that seem more dramatic. In fact, the small deeds may well be more disruptive to your own world and even less easily repaid. And since no one else knows you did them, you won't even get the recognition that comes with the more dramatic forms of hospitality. Yet they carry the same risk that someone might take advantage of you and your kindness.

Now, just a word of caution about taking risks: hospitality is not the same as letting someone run over you. While hospitality is willing to take the risk of being used, it doesn't keep taking it when the other person has shown only an interest in using you. There comes a point where you have to ask, "What kind of aid am I offering? Does my hospitality help someone get back on her feet, or does my help allow someone else to stay immature, wrongly sponging off others?"

Having said that, I'm still concerned if our first response is to fear being taken advantage of, because I think there's an even greater danger. Why do we so easily assume that the danger of being ripped off is greater than the danger of ignoring God's blessing? Remember the incentive found in the second half of Hebrews 13:2: "Do not neglect to show hospitality to strangers, for thereby some have entertained angels unawares"?

If you have the possibility of entertaining angels, it's not because they're coming to you on their own initiative. It would be because God sent them. Therefore, they—or others needing your help—will be at your door only at his direction. That's helpful to me. When I consider taking a risk to help someone, I like to know that this is not a freak accident of timing, but that God has been involved in us crossing paths, just as surely as he was out in the vastness of the desert where he made sure his path crossed with Abraham's.

Please don't miss God's intention of blessing you through the strangers he sends you. As many times as I've heard—or verbalized—concerns and warnings regarding being taken advantage of, I have yet to hear anyone capture the essence of this verse by saying, "Oh, I am so concerned that I might miss an opportunity to provide for someone in Jesus' name!" I haven't even heard the more self-serving version: "I don't want to miss the chance to host messengers of God who will surely be as much of a blessing to me as I will to them!"

As with everything else in life, my fears and confidences in this area reflect my experience of the gospel. If I am hyper-afraid of being ripped off, then I don't really believe I have a gracious, generous God who has brought me into the richness of his family. But if I know that God has welcomed me to experience his riches, I care much less if someone ends up stealing from me.

In that respect, hospitality is more than a gamble on whether God may or may not bless you—hospitality sits at the heart of the gospel. And the gospel is the great equalizer between you and someone who might be tempted to abuse your kindness.

Jesus Already Took the Biggest Hospitality Risk

Consider how you first came to Jesus. Didn't it involve some level of your own self-serving felt needs? For many years the thing I wanted most was to avoid hell. I didn't come to Jesus solely because I longed for the glory of God to cover the earth as the waters cover the sea. I didn't come because I just couldn't stand the thought of not being with him. I came with my own agenda and my own beliefs regarding what I needed, and therefore, I came because of what I wanted from him.

So have many people . . . er, most people? . . . all people? Some come because they don't want to be lonely. Other people are tired of their life not working well and hope that maybe Jesus can make things run more smoothly. Others just want to stop feeling guilty, or to belong to a healthy community, or be taken care of. The list of impure and mixed motives is endless.

Amazingly, Jesus is *still* hospitable to us. He opens the doors of his home to us even while we're thinking about how we can get enough of his goodies to satisfy our souls. We're like a pack of street urchins who are invited into a mansion of a man wealthy beyond our imagination. The home is neat, orderly, and happy. We can see how fine and grand everything is and how it's all simply a warm-up to the main event—to get to meet the owner of such a place! When we do meet him, he smiles and welcomes us. He embraces us and invites us to sit down at a table of the most wonderful food imaginable, then promises us a bath afterward, a game to enjoy, and deep rest in the best bed money can buy.

All the while, we're not enamored with him. Sure, we're smart enough to give him some of our attention, but we slyly peek around at his stuff, measuring it with our eyes to see if maybe we could pocket it to sell later. And he knows it. We're not fooling him. He's onto our tricks and more than aware that his stuff captures us more than he does. But he doesn't throw us out. Instead, he adopts us so that everything he has becomes ours. In doing that, he changes our hearts, just as surely as Valjean's changed. The joke is on us. The thief becomes family because the Father risks being taken advantage of.

That's what you're doing in your relationships when you interrupt your schedule and comforts for someone else. You're inviting people to form much deeper connections with you even if initially all that captured their attention was the thing you offered to them to meet their need.

Hospitality Shows Your Experience of the Gospel

Caring for strangers in their distress is a direct expression of the way that God has dealt with you. "For you know the grace of our Lord Jesus Christ, that though he was rich, yet for your sake he became poor, so that you by his poverty might become rich" (2 Corinthians 8:9).

Surrounded by more and better riches than you literally can imagine, Jesus gave up all he had to come find you so you could share in those riches with him. *Your* hospitality, then, is a sermon in pictures for the rest of the world to stand back and ponder. When you give away the things you have to enrich someone who is poor, you proclaim the heart of what drives your God.

Yes, the things you give are helpful in and of themselves, but the activity of giving is far more valuable. Doing so paints a small picture of something beyond yourself. It depicts the greater reality of a God who has sought you out to give you the glory of heaven. Hospitality is a Christian virtue precisely because it's a reflection of how God has responded to you as a stranger in need. It's one way that you express how you have experienced the gospel.

Karl remained grateful his whole life. A German-born Jew, he fled Nazi Germany before the beginning of the Second World War. Arriving in the United States with nothing, he was welcomed into a college fraternity that housed and fed him while he completed his studies. Karl never forgot the kindness he was shown. Instead, he felt a keen desire to pass along the goodness he received. So he and his wife built an apartment for students that they offered at a greatly reduced rate. His hospitality was induced by what he experienced from ordinary people. How much greater should ours be, considering what we have experienced from Jesus?

The reality of Christ extending himself to you undergirds your hospitable impulse, but it also reveals what is heinous about being inhospitable. When you sit back, believing that it's someone else's responsibility to help, or when you try to manage people's needs instead of meeting them, you show how little appreciation you have for Christ's hospitality. Sure, you're happy enough that Jesus became poor so you might become rich, but in the moment that you're not happy to give what you have to help someone else, you deny the gospel. You proclaim a god who is stingy, hoarding, and desperately trying to hold onto the few pennies he has left. You proclaim a god who cannot afford to be ripped off or taken advantage of, who needs a guaranteed return on his investment or all of heaven will collapse.

When you understand that your experience of the gospel underlies your hospitality (or lack thereof), you are better prepared to understand the parable of the sheep and the goats. In Matthew 25:31–46 Jesus teaches that at the end of time people will be rewarded or punished according to what they've done for the poor and needy. While there is no overt mention of grace in this particular passage, Leon Morris goes to the heart of it when he notes that, "The works we do are the evidence of the grace of God at work in us or the rejection of that grace."[1] Our expression of human hospitality shows our experience of divine hospitality.

If you have no impulse to be hospitable to the needy or reach out to help the people closest to you, then you show you have no awareness of your own great need or any experience of receiving God's hospitality. When you extend hospitality to the hungry, thirsty, homeless, naked, sick or imprisoned, you are acknowledging that you at one time were impoverished, unable to help yourself.

At that time, Jesus came and fed you, invited you in, clothed you, and rescued you. In turn, you are so amazed that you would be sought out and cared for that you gladly delight to give that experience to others without thinking that you have done anything special. And in doing so, you learn at the end of days that you have been entertaining not simply humans, nor even angels unawares, but the Lord himself.

On Your Own

1. What keeps you from being more hospitable? What thoughts run through your mind when you're faced with a need you don't want to meet? What fears hold you back? Do you tend to be more driven by self-protection or unwillingness? How do you justify this unwillingness to yourself?

2. How well do you regularly see Christ's hospitality to you—that though he was rich, yet for your sake he became poor? Where have you experienced him caring for your needs this past week?

3. When was the last time you showed hospitality and expected nothing back or freely gave to someone who couldn't return the favor? Why did you do so? What blessings did you receive from the Lord?

4. Showing hospitality unexpectedly often requires preparation to be ready when the need arises. What lifestyle decisions do you need to make to be ready for those moments when they arise? How familiar are you with the human services agencies in your area? The more prepared you are, the better you will be able to serve, which makes it more likely that God will send people your way.

Guaranteed to Love

What do you think of this rare jewel of love we've been exploring? We've learned so much by turning it over and looking at a few of its facets, but there is much more richness still to discover and enjoy as you live among God's people. We've only begun to explore God's love.

It reminds me of being alongside the ocean. I grew up on the northeastern seaboard, so I've had the privilege of being able to go to the shore regularly. It's my favorite place on earth. One kitschy placard captures my sentiments exactly: "If you're lucky enough to be at the beach, then you're lucky enough." I don't care what time of year it is, every time we go I can hardly wait. It never gets old or loses its allure.

That's beginning to surprise me. After more than four decades of beach trips, I am amazed that I see something new each time, something I've never seen before—an unusual shell, an odd plant, a fish gliding through or arcing out of the water, a different kind of bird, a creature burrowed into the sand, or some new confluence of waves and wind. The ocean's biodiversity is vast beyond my imagining. I wonder what you would find if you plunged into its ecosystem and studied it systematically, rather than simply noticing what you come across accidentally while standing at its edge?

Exploring love is like that too. There's always something new to discover. I suspect, since love is part of God's DNA, that it is as varied and limitless as he himself is. Our time together in these pages is barely enough to get us started investigating something that will literally take forever to adequately grasp.

However, this time might have been long enough to overwhelm or discourage you more than it thrilled you. As glorious as love is and as important as it is to God's family, most of my friends and I still struggle to see its reality lived out in our lives. It is so much easier to find examples of things we do that are dark or unpleasant.

At least, that's what Brandon believed as he regretted all the ways he was mean-spirited and angry at his family, driving them away. His failings were far more obvious to him than his successes. Tears came to his eyes repeatedly as he wrestled with feelings of hopelessness that he would ever grow into the gentle, kind, longsuffering, patient man in his home that he longed to be.

Can you relate?

Life is hard and our responses to it are not always up to the challenge. Our failures become more obvious as the Spirit of God shines his light into the dark corners of our lives. But there are reasons for you to hold onto hope that goes deeper than any despair you might have. If you're discouraged over how poorly you love others or how little you experience love, step back and take in the long view.

Sin and suffering will pass. For me, at most, I'm looking at no more than fifty more years of sin and suffering. That's really short compared to the next 27 billion years I'm anticipating (that is, the front end of eternity). In a brief century the ugly realities you wrestle with now will no longer be part of your life. But love will be.

A perfect you will continue to live—in perfect friendships with a perfect God among his perfect family. And love will be at the heart of those relationships. The small steps you take now to learn and practice love will set your feet on a forever path that will leave your failures in the forgotten dust. You will quickly find it easier to run down this path than the dark ones you now frequent because this is a spirit-empowered path.

Look to Jesus When You Lose Confidence

You'll gain even more confidence to take those steps as you meditate on what Jesus came to earth to accomplish. Do you remember when he told his disciples, "By this all people will know that you are my disciples, if you have love for one another" (John 13:35)? If you're skeptical about your ability to live this out today, realize that the first disciples had as much reason to be skeptical. The bar Jesus raised was as daunting for them two thousand years ago as it is for us today. Certainly they had their share of experiences that would lead them to believe they had little hope of living well with each other.

How could it be that they would be marked by the quality of their love? It was going to be true because Jesus had already come to love them into a new experience. Not just talk to them about love, but actually love them. They had already experienced and would continue to experience the very best relationship they were ever going to have—with him. And as they mined the riches of that relationship, they would have more than enough to give away to others.

You will too.

Jesus is not content to watch people created in his image live isolated, lonely lives after humanity's rebellion against him. He longs for his creatures to enjoy satisfying relationships that reflect the goodness of what he experiences as a member of the Trinity.

He is so committed to this goal that he gave up all that was comfortable in order to make his hopes and dreams for his people reality. Can you imagine him giving up all that if it was only for the mere *chance* of making things different? No. He's better and wiser than that. He sacrificed in order to ensure that his plans became reality.

As Brandon and I talked, I asked him about his experience raising his own children. I said, "You took a risk when you decided to have your son, didn't you? You were excited and happy, but there was probably some nervousness too because you didn't know what he was going to be like. But you decided to have him anyway and love him through his difficult moments."

Brandon smiled and agreed, so I continued. "I know you love your son, but I also know he can make you nuts at times. Would you have been as quick to want him if you knew that he was going to lie to you and defy you 873 times . . . before he was thirteen?"

This time he smiled more broadly. "Well, maybe not."

"That's where God is different," I said. "He knew all about you and all about your failures. How you wouldn't love your family well or be good to them, and he still wanted you—with a smile on his face. He looked down eternity from where he sat and decided he would rather die than not have you . . . so he did." Brandon picked up his head.

I continued, "God didn't risk a thing. He knew exactly what he was getting and decided you were worth what it would cost him. Do you really think he's tired of you and ready to be done with you? You are absolutely going to overcome these things, and you don't have to wait until eternity to get started. You will learn to love your family, not because you're so wonderful, but because he knows what he's doing."

That's true not only for Brandon, but for you and me too. Our God does not blindly hope he'll be happy with the results of his actions. He acts because he knows with certainty that he will be completely satisfied for all eternity. That means we have an iron-clad, rock-solid guarantee. You and I are becoming experts in loving others.

Count on it.

Notes

CHAPTER 1: COMFORTING LOVE

1. My thanks to my lead pastor and friend Reverend Andy Hudson for first drawing my attention to this focus in Isaiah 53.

CHAPTER 2: SYMPATHETIC LOVE

1. Joni Eareckson-Tada and Steve Estes do a compelling job presenting God's claim to be sovereign over all suffering while also being deeply touched by it in *When God Weeps: Why Our Sufferings Matter to the Almighty* (Grand Rapids, MI: Zondervan, 1997). See especially their appendices for an extensive list of scriptural supports. The specific passage I've reworded comes from page 115.
2. Much of what I know of this passage I've learned from my colleague, mentor, and friend, Paul Tripp.
3. William L. Lane, *Word Biblical Commentary: Hebrews 1–8,* 47A (Dallas, TX: Word Books, 1991), 108. As William Lane explains, sympathy in this verse "means to share the experience of someone."

CHAPTER 4: FORGIVING LOVE

1. Ezekiel 28:11–19 in the context of Revelation 12:7–12 and Jude 6.
2. For more development of this idea see my minibook, *When Bad Things Happen* (Greensboro, NC: New Growth Press, 2008).

CHAPTER 5: LONGSUFFERING LOVE

1. My debt for these two words, along with some of my understanding of the function of covenant meals, goes to Peter Enns from his commentary

on Exodus (*Exodus: NIV Application Commentary* [Grand Rapids: Zondervan, 2000], 492).

CHAPTER 9: SERVING LOVE

1. Although animal waste is not explicitly cited in the text, I don't believe it requires much imagination to realize that livestock would use the same roadways—especially on the way to the temple in Jerusalem—and that with livestock come certain "by-products." My description is admittedly a dramatized reconstruction, but that's not the same as saying it's groundless fiction. Rather, it seems to me that more than mere dust would have to be involved in order to generate the deep contempt associated with foot-washing or loosing sandals. Such contempt suggests that my inference is more than plausible. See for example: Andreas J. Köstenberger, *John* (Grand Rapids, MI: Baker Academic, 2004), 403–5; Bruce Milne, *The Message of John: Here is Your King!* (Downers Grove, IL: Inter-Varsity, 1993), 52 and 196; Leon Morris, *The Gospel According to John, Revised* (Grand Rapids, MI: William B. Eerdmans, 1995), 124.
2. See for example, D.A. Carson, *The Gospel According to John* (Grand Rapids, MI: William B. Eerdmans, 1991), 462.
3. My thanks to Brad Beevers, who pointed this out to me years ago.
4. I am indebted to Brooke Solberg for drawing my attention to the spirituality of sharpening pencils.

CHAPTER 10: PROVIDING LOVE

1. I am also deeply grateful for the countless and costly contributions of many people in helping us (re)build our home. I am so thankful for the friends and family who donated hours, expertise, and finances to gut rooms, run electric wires, redo the heating/air-conditioning system, straighten out the plumbing, repair the roof, landscape the yard, and so on. Thankfully I will never be able to brag about "the house that Bill built," because without everyone else, it would not have been.
2. For example, see Luke 24:13–35, especially v. 27; and John 5:36–47, especially vv. 39 and 46.

CHAPTER 11: WELCOMING LOVE

1. I am indebted to David Powlison for providing the catalyst for the following thoughts.
2. The two speakers are distinguished by paying attention to the male and female pronouns used at various times throughout the Song.

CHAPTER 12: HUMBLE LOVE

1. Andrew T. Lincoln, *Ephesians* (Dallas: Word Books, 1990), 351.
2. See Abraham bartering with God over Sodom and Gomorrah (Genesis 18:22–33), Hezekiah being granted an extra fifteen years of life because of his tearful prayer (2 Kings 20:1–11), or Ezekiel getting to cook his food over a fuel source that wouldn't make him unclean (Ezekiel 4, especially verses 12–15).
3. For a longer discussion of this argument and its place within the book of Ephesians, see my article, "Culture: Hate It? Love It? . . . Redeem It!" *Journal of Biblical Counseling,* 22, no. 2, (2004): 2–14, specifically pp. 9–10 under the subheading "6. Moral Standards."

CHAPTER 14: PEACEFUL LOVE

1. This quotation is taken from *The Oxford Dictionary of Modern Quotations* (*http://theoxforddictionaryofmodernquotations.blogspot.com/2008/06/oxford-dictionary-of-modern-quotations_25.html,* accessed: May 10, 2011), which references it as, "Speech from window of 10 Downing Street, 30 Sept. 1938, in *The Times* 1 Oct. 1938."
2. (*http://www.facebook.com/JimiHendrixFoundation* accessed: May 10, 2011).
3. (*http://www.dalailamafoundation.org/dlf/en/youth4outlooks.jsp,* accessed: May 10, 2011)

CHAPTER 15: HOSPITABLE LOVE

1. Leon Morris, *The Gospel According to Matthew* (Grand Rapids, MI: William B. Eerdmans, 1992), 634.

Index of Scripture